C000132818

Agricultural Growth for the Poor: An Agenda for Development

THE WORLD BANK
Washington, D.C.

ISBN: 0-8213-6067-1
EAN: 978-0-8213-6067-5
e-ISBN: 0-8213-6068-X

Library of Congress cataloging-in-publication data has been applied for.

Cover photo: World Bank.

Contents

Tables

Boxes

Foreword

Broad-based agricultural development on small farms has been a powerful force for promoting growth and reducing poverty in many poor countries. Support for agriculture has been especially beneficial in countries where large numbers of people earn a living as farmers or landless laborers. Agricultural development has often stimulated growth that extends well beyond rural areas—over the past decades, higher incomes from agriculture and access to cheaper food have helped hundreds of millions of people to move beyond living on less than US$1 per day.

The resolution to halve the number of people suffering from extreme hunger and poverty by 2015 is first on the list of Millennium Development Goals (MDGs) adopted by the international community. In many low-income countries, the level of support provided by governments and donors to agriculture will largely determine whether this goal is achieved. Agriculture will also play a crucial part in realizing the MDGs of gender equality and environmental sustainability.

There is no guarantee that agriculture's remarkable success in reversing poverty and fostering other development objectives will persist. For better or worse, the agricultural context in many developing countries is far different from what it was even a decade ago. Agriculture presents a series of significant new challenges and opportunities that will require more innovative, decentralized, and inclusive approaches to development, from farmers' fields to the national and international forums where policies and investments traditionally have been determined. For example:

- urbanization and trade are transforming the food supply chain from producers to consumers;
- prices of traditional cereal crops and traditional export commodities, the mainstay of hundreds of millions of poor producers, have fallen dramatically;
- farmers face radical new demands with respect to the quality and traceability of their produce; and
- environmental challenges have multiplied.

As countries diversify, urbanize, and industrialize, support to agriculture by the donor community and governments themselves has steadily declined over the past two decades. Agriculture will survive, of course. A growing population has to be fed, and rising incomes will create new opportunities for rural households. But who will make a good living in agriculture in the years to come, producing what products, with what technologies, and for what markets? Will small farms prosper? Will poor rural households, especially in harsh environments, be drawn into a widening set of economic opportunities? Will the growth impetus of agriculture endure? This report describes what governments, international agencies, rural people, the private sector, and others can do to ensure that these challenges can be met and that critical opportunities for progress toward the MDGs are not lost.

Kevin Cleaver
Director
Agriculture and Rural
   Development Department

Sushma Ganguly
Sector Manager
Agriculture and Rural
   Development Department

Acknowledgments

Preparation of this report has been managed by the Agriculture and Rural Development Department. Derek Byerlee, Cees de Haan, Sam Kane, Eija Pehu, Cathy Ragasa, and Alex Winters-Nelson wrote the report, with inputs from Kees van der Meer, Laura Ignacio, John Nash, Ulrich Hess, Renate Kloeppinger-Todd, Jock Anderson, Shawki Barghouti, Ariel Dinar, Salah Darghouth, Erick Fernandes, Lynn Brown, Riikka Rajalahti, Nwanze Okidegbe, Neil MacPherson, Felicity Proctor, Severin Kodderitzsch, Arunima Dhar, and Gary Alex. Kelly Cassaday greatly improved readability, and many others provided support, including Fleurdeliza Canlas, Sarian Akibo-Betts, Jonathan Agwe, Sanjiva Cooke, Corazon Solomon, and Melissa Williams. The report was reviewed by Akin Adesina, Simon Maxwell, Rita Sharma, Wally Tyner, Robert Townsend, and Dina Umali-Deininger; comments were received from many others, including Astrid Agostini, Samuel Jutzi, Andrew McMillan, Michael Wales, and other colleagues at FAO. The Department for International Development of the United Kingdom supported background analytical work for the report.

Kevin Cleaver and Sushma Ganguly have provided invaluable support throughout the development of this report. Their contributions have lent clarity and power to a document that is intended to support the development community in its efforts to put a new public policy agenda to work for agriculture and the poor.

Derek Byerlee
Adviser,
Rural Policy and Strategy
Agricultural and Rural
 Development

Eija Pehu
Adviser,
Science and Technology
Agricultural and Rural
 Development

Acronyms

AAPP	African Agricultural Productivity Program
AICHA	Agricultural Initiative to Cut Hunger in Africa
AFR	Africa Region
APL	adjustable program loan
CDD	community-driven development
CGIAR	Consultative Group on International Agricultural Research
CIAL	Local Agricultural Research Committee
CIAT	International Center for Tropical Agriculture
CIDR	International Center for Development Banks
CODEX	The Codex Alimentarius Commission
CVECA	Self-Managed Village Savings and Credit Banks
DFID	U.K. Department for International Development
EAP	East Asia and the Pacific Region
EBS	Equity Building Society
ECA	Europe and Central Asia Region
ESSD	economically and socially sustainable development
EU	European Union
FAO	Food and Agriculture Organization of the United Nations
GDP	gross domestic product
GEF	Global Environmental Facility
HACCP	hazard analysis and critical control points
ICRW	International Center for Research on Women
IFAD	International Fund for Agricultural Development
IFC	International Finance Corporation
IFDC	International Fertilizer Development Center
IFPRI	International Food Policy Research Institute
IIED	International Institute for Environment and Development
IITA	International Institute of Tropical Agriculture
IPM	integrated pest management
IPPC	International Plant Protection Convention
IPRs	intellectual property rights
LAC	Latin America and the Carribbean Region
LEAD	Livestock, Environment, and Development Initiative
LEISA	low external input and sustainable agriculture

LIL	learning and innovation loan
MAPP	Multi-Country Agricultural Productivity Program
MDGs	Millennium Development Goals
MFIs	microfinance institutions
MNA	Middle and North Asia Region
MRL	maximum residue levels
NAFTA	North American Free Trade Agreement
NARF	National Agricultural Research Fund
NEPAD	New Partnership for Africa's Development
NERICA	New Rice for Africa
NGO	nongovernmental organization
NRDP	Northeast Rural Development Program
NRM	natural resource management
ODA	official development assistance
ODI	Overseas Development Institute
OECD	Organisation for Economic Co-operation and Development
OED	Operations Evaluation Department (of the World Bank)
OIE	Office International des Épizooties
PIM	participatory irrigation management
PROCAMPO	Program for Direct Assistance to Agriculture
PRSC	Poverty Reduction Support Credit
PRSP	Poverty Reduction Strategy Paper
PSAL	programmatic sector adjustment loan
RPOs	rural producer organizations
R&D	research and development
SAL	sector adjustment loan
SAS	South Asia
SILs	sector investment loans
SMEs	small and medium enterprises
SPS	sanitary and phytosanitary
SWAp	sectorwide approach
TAL	technical assitance loan
USAID	U.S. Agency for International Development
WEHAB	water, energy, health, agriculture, and biodiversity
WHO	World Health Organization
WTO	World Trade Organization
WUAs	water user associations

Executive Summary

The potential and the urgency for securing agriculture's prominence in the development agenda have never been greater. A series of global challenges and opportunities, from the biophysical forces driving climate change to the complex rules governing markets and trade, are rapidly defining an entirely new set of conditions for agriculture. At the same time, the international community is confronting the escalating social and economic costs of poverty, hunger, gender inequality, environmental degradation, and other barriers to development—many of which can be addressed by agricultural growth that benefits the poor.

The majority of the world's poor depend directly or indirectly on agriculture. Many impoverished people have benefited from the substantial investments made in agricultural development in the 1970s and 1980s. These investments brought major breakthroughs to farmers' fields, enabling countries to improve food security, increase the incomes of rural households, and use agriculture as the engine of growth for the whole economy. Over the past decade, the global population living on less than US$1 per day has fallen from 28 to 22 percent, an achievement that owes a great deal to increased incomes from agriculture. Increased food production has also reduced malnourishment for hundreds of millions of people.

Missed Connections: Has the World Forgotten Agriculture's Role in Development?

Despite the strong connections between broad-based agricultural growth, overall economic growth, and poverty reduction, international support to agriculture has declined sharply since the late 1980s. Many factors contributed to this decline: increased competition for resources from priorities emerging in other sectors; an unwillingness to make the long-term commitment required for agricultural development; the high costs, complexity, and risks of some types of agricultural support; and the under-representation of rural people in political processes.

Yet broad-based agricultural growth in low-income countries is essential to reach the Millennium Development Goal (MDG) of halving the number of people in extreme poverty and cutting hunger in half by 2015. Moreover, agriculture is a crucial sector for realizing the MDGs of gender equality and environmental sustainability. Nowhere are these challenges

greater than in Sub-Saharan Africa, where the number of poor people
increased by 34 percent between 1990 and 2000.

A New Rural Development Strategy

The World Bank's rural development strategy, *Reaching the Rural Poor*,
approved in 2003, recognizes that agricultural growth is central to reducing poverty. It acknowledges that outmoded approaches to supporting
agriculture must give way to new approaches that reflect rapid changes
in the global environment for agriculture and economic growth. Together
with its companion publication, the *Agriculture Investment Sourcebook*, this
report seeks to strengthen the implementation of the World Bank's rural
development strategy by:

- reviewing the strong case for *increased international support* for agriculture to reduce poverty and contribute to the MDGs (chapter 1);
- describing the *changing global context* that will shape strategies to foster
  growth and enable the poor to participate in emerging market opportunities (chapter 2);
- providing an overview of key *policy and institutional issues* involved in
  accelerating growth to benefit the poor, with an emphasis on creating
  an *enabling environment* for the private sector (chapter 3);
- articulating *priorities for public investment* in agriculture and describing
  innovative partnerships for the public sector, private sector (including
  farmers), and civil society to enhance the impact of public expenditures
  (chapter 4);
- highlighting the need to *tailor strategies* to specific agricultural contexts, defined by agroclimatic and socioeconomic features (chapter 5);
  and
- demonstrating how support for agriculture from the Bank and its partners can lead to *better lending* that is more fully integrated into country-
  wide strategies and new lending instruments (chapter 6).

The report also summarizes what has been learned about successful
support to agricultural development, presents cases that highlight specific good practices, and discusses areas that should be scaled up and
areas where more learning is required.

Rapid Global Change in Agricultural Markets

Strategies for promoting agricultural development that benefits the poor
must enable agriculture to adjust to the rapidly changing global scene,
both on the demand and supply side of agricultural markets.

- *On the demand side,* prices for many traditional commodities continue to decline because of rapid productivity growth in some countries, static demand, and heavy subsidies imposed on some commodities by countries belonging to the Organisation for Economic Co-operation and Development (OECD). At the same time, however, growth in consumer incomes and growing demand from world markets for higher value products are opening new opportunities for agriculture in the developing world. These changing demand patterns are transforming the food system, generating new technical and institutional challenges for coordination along the market chain to control quality and enter new markets. These changes present special challenges for smallholders' participation in these markets, although potentially negative effects on the poor are often offset by increased employment in agribusiness and by lower food costs.
- *On the supply side,* advances in science and knowledge drive agriculture far more than they did in the past, when increasing land, water, and levels of other inputs were the major sources of growth. Exponential progress in molecular biology and information technology promises to raise yields for farmers in developing countries and at the same time alter global patterns of competitive advantage. Growing evidence of resource degradation in high-potential and more marginal agricultural areas presents major challenges to developing and disseminating agricultural practices that sustain the natural resource base. Agricultural development programs also must take account of dramatic demographic change. In many middle-income countries, people leave poverty behind by leaving agriculture behind, which raises rural wages but also leaves an aging rural population. In Africa, rural populations are being devastated by HIV/AIDS, with its disastrous impacts on households and agricultural labor. Finally, agriculture is especially affected by increasingly extreme and erratic weather. The frequency of droughts and flooding is expected to increase, and reduced rainfall and higher temperatures due to global warming will negatively affect food production in the tropics.

Harnessing Change to Benefit the Poor: Priorities for Public Support to Agriculture

To harness powerful global changes in ways that benefit the poor, the World Bank and its partners are changing their priorities for supporting agriculture. Priorities to support the agricultural sector include: (1) fostering the provision of global public goods and services, (2) accelerating policy reforms, (3) developing institutions to support the private sector, (4) fostering decentralization and empowerment of the poor, and

(5) investing in core public goods that strengthen physical, human, natural, and social capital.

Fostering the Provision of Global Public Goods and Services

Globalization is leading to greater interdependency between countries and to the development of international agreements and treaties that govern the provision of regional and global public goods and services. These agreements, which are especially important in agriculture, increasingly regulate agricultural activities involving common resources, protect intellectual property rights, promote collective action in areas such as agricultural research and development (R&D), and regulate global markets. The World Bank has identified three priority global activities:

- *Advocacy to level the playing field in agricultural trade:* There is a continuous need for advocacy to reduce trade-distorting agricultural subsidies and to strengthen developing countries' negotiating position in trade agreements. The World Bank will continue to raise awareness of the serious impact of trade-distorting subsidies on small-scale producers and processors in the developing world. It will support ways of strengthening developing countries' negotiating position in trade agreements, and it will conduct more in-depth analytical work to assess how subsidies and protection affect specific commodities that are important for small-scale producers in developing countries.
- *Continued support for international agricultural research:* The international community's investment in the research centers supported by the Consultative Group on International Agricultural Research (CGIAR) has significantly reduced poverty. Support for international agricultural research through the CGIAR must be sustained. This support will ensure that the CGIAR continues to focus on international public goods of most benefit to the poor and that it secures partnerships with the private sector to gain free or low-cost access to the new scientific tools that are critical for solving problems faced by poor farmers.
- *More attention to climate change:* The importance of global climate change for agriculture requires increased analytical work and capacity building that will help agriculture mitigate and adjust to the effects of global warming.

Accelerating Policy Reforms

Policy reform has occurred more slowly in agriculture than in other sectors. High levels of protection of agricultural imports, taxes on agricultural exports, and continued public intervention in input and output markets are undermining the competitive position of many countries. Key areas for policy reform are:

- **Trade liberalization:** Even as negotiations intended to reduce distortions in world trade continue, there is much that the individual developing countries can do to reform their own trade policies. Although there is a growing body of evidence to show that trade liberalization is beneficial to the poor in the long run, more can be learned about sequencing reforms in a way that minimizes adverse effects on the economy in the short term and supports vulnerable groups that may be negatively affected. There is no one-size-fits-all approach to trade liberalization. Reforms must be designed to fit the specific conditions of each country.
- **Market reforms:** In many cases, the private sector has successfully replaced inefficient public or parastatal agencies in supplying essentially private services, including the distribution of agricultural inputs and the processing and marketing of farm products. In others, however, further liberalization of domestic markets is needed to encourage private investment and provision of services. Market reforms have sometimes been implemented before the private sector gained the capacity to step in when public companies were closed. Policies to liberalize or privatize marketing functions must be sequentially implemented over time to ensure that the institutional framework for competitive markets develops, that support services are in place during the transition, and that complementary investments are made that enable the private sector to function smoothly.
- **Changing public and private sector roles:** Governments were once active in production, processing, and trade, but the rise of supply chains and the application of more rigid grades and standards will require governments to act more as facilitators that develop and enforce the rules by which private sector participants interact within market arenas. *Although current development strategies provide for increased private sector leadership, it must not be forgotten that the quality and efficiency of public policies, institutions, and investments are increasingly critical for the emergence of a competitive agricultural sector.* Many government functions can be contracted out to specialized private firms and nongovernmental organizations (NGOs) under competitive bidding. Governments must also increasingly partner with the private sector and civil society—including producer organizations, water user associations, NGOs, and trade associations—in areas such as policy analysis, food safety regulation, and the provision of infrastructure and irrigation.

Developing Institutions to Support the Private Sector

Institutions and corresponding investments should promote sustained private investment that also benefits the poor by providing for:

- *An appropriate regulatory environment for the private sector to grow:* The public sector's direct role in markets is decreasing, but the development of private markets depends on whether the public sector can provide an effective and streamlined regulatory environment, including specifications for grades and standards as well as food safety, biosafety, and environmental protection. An effective regulatory environment lowers transaction costs, reduces the risk of doing business, and improves the marketability of products. A special challenge is to prevent standards from reflecting wealthy countries' interests and becoming major barriers to trade. An important opportunity for donor support is presented by current discussions of standards to be included in sanitary and phytosanitary (SPS) agreements. Developing countries could benefit both from support in negotiating these standards and from developing the infrastructure (e.g., laboratories) they need to comply with them.
- *Agricultural innovation systems:* The World Bank has extensive experience in developing and evaluating good practice in agricultural innovation systems. Those systems are more likely to be effective if they follow a flexible institutional model that features greater participation of universities and the private sector, public-private partnerships, and strong participation of users in setting the research agenda. Although there is less experience with new models for agricultural advisory services, there is growing evidence that decentralized systems have significant benefits, especially if they involve the private sector and civil society and establish incentive systems based largely on the private provision of services. However, innovation systems will require continuing strong public support, especially in poorer regions and countries.
- *Agricultural finance:* The current priority for public policy is to create the conditions under which financial institutions and markets can grow, rather than to provide credit directly for agriculture. New models, which encompass a range of financial services and risk management instruments, appear promising. Innovative microfinance institutions in the rural sector have helped smallholders, particularly the poor and women, expand their productive activities. Agricultural finance remains an area of continuous learning and experimentation, as the World Bank seeks to develop effective instruments for working with the private sector.

- *Managing risk and vulnerability:* Poor farmers are especially vulnerable to agroclimatic shocks (e.g., droughts or plant disease epidemics) and to extreme fluctuations in commodity prices, but new market-based tools are emerging to supplement and strengthen the ways that governments and households manage risks. A recent innovation for price hedging, being piloted in developing countries, uses futures options to lock in prices and facilitate access to credit for small-scale producers of coffee and other products. Another recently developed market instrument is index-based crop or livestock insurance, which uses an insurance trigger that cannot be manipulated by the insured (e.g., a weather index). While these instruments show promise, key questions remain about how public-private partnerships can reduce the costs of making such risk management tools available to small-scale farmers.
- *Secure access to land and water:* Secure land and water rights are essential to foster growth that benefits the poor. The World Bank and its partners are scaling up efforts to secure land rights, including the formal recognition of customary systems and the establishment of efficient land administration systems. In areas where land ownership is extremely unequal, community-based models for land redistribution, coupled with strong support by local governments and NGOs, show promise. Given the growing scarcity of water, the development of parallel private markets for water presents a major challenge in many countries. Gender inequities are also commonly encountered with respect to land and water rights, and these are now being addressed in World Bank operations.

Fostering Decentralization and Empowerment of the Poor

A continuing high priority is to shift responsibility and capacity for delivering services to the local level and to increase the participation of disadvantaged groups in making decisions, shaping public interventions to local conditions, and improving the accountability of service providers. Institutions for empowerment and decentralization are particularly important to catalyze demand for the research and extension services that will ensure that producers have the knowledge and skills to adapt to market opportunities and environmental constraints.

By forming strong organizations, smallholders can manage resources more efficiently and participate more readily in new production and marketing arrangements. The formation of local water user associations (WUAs) to operate and manage irrigation systems has often proven to be the most important step in improving and sustaining irrigation systems. There are now many examples of small-scale producers organizing to supply higher-value crops for international markets. Trade associations and producer cooperatives also have a role in improving coordination along the supply chain and in communicating the needs of an industry to government. Capacity building for producer organizations is being mainstreamed in World Bank lending operations. Currently 40 percent of World Bank agricultural projects involve such associations.

Investing in Core Public Goods and Stimulating Market Development

Public investments are needed to support core public goods related to infrastructure, natural resources, technology, and information, and to strengthen physical, human, and social capital. The development community has considerable experience with investments in most of these public goods, and investments can now be scaled up. Areas that require additional learning and evaluation include agricultural education (increasingly urgent as agriculture becomes more knowledge-intensive) and the management of overexploited communal natural resources, such as arid and semiarid rangelands.

Much has also been learned about investment instruments and approaches that encourage partnerships between the public and the private sectors to promote poor people's access to assets and markets. Time-limited investments and matching grants are increasingly used for (1) activities with a high impact on poverty reduction, especially in marginal areas, to support poor people's access to land and water and reduce risk and vulnerability; and (2) activities that support private sector and market development and have significant additional benefits, such as training, technology development, access to information, project preparation, investment in local infrastructure, and collective action for mutual benefit. When deciding on the entry points, continuing attention must be given to: (1) the fine line between public sector support and public sector interference; (2) the large diversity of needs in relation to specific approaches; and (3) the most effective way of leveraging private sector resources. Good practice is still evolving on ways to build public agencies' capacity to identify, target, and implement useful interventions in partnership with others in ways that are nondistorting, market-oriented, and capable of generating net benefits to the poor over the long term.

Agriculture and the Environment

Agriculture can have major positive and negative effects on the environment. For example, agricultural intensification can reduce the clearing of forested land but it can also increase pollution from pesticides or large-

scale livestock production. Often a first step in avoiding negative externalities is to remove subsidies on activities that cause them, especially
input subsidies. Incentives can also be provided to implement resource-
conserving technologies such as better watershed management practices
or conservation tillage practices. Another promising approach is to tax
polluting activities so that farmers can be paid to use techniques that protect the environment. There are some prospects for rural people to provide environmental services, especially in marginal drylands where the
potential for agriculture is often limited and few alternatives exist.

Adjusting Support to Diverse Conditions

Policy and investment priorities must be tailored to specific agricultural
production systems. The great diversity of agricultural systems can make
this a daunting task, but major commonalities in production systems can
be used to classify systems and to identify and prioritize the few elements
that are most critical to overcoming key constraints on development in
each one. Examples are given for three agricultural mega-systems:

- *In irrigated high-potential areas,* which have good infrastructure, the
  most important strategy is to diversify on and off of the farm. On the
  farm, higher value products can be produced. Off of the farm, diversification presents new opportunities for adding value, and industrialization creates employment opportunities that spill into rural areas.
  Growth in high-potential areas is driven basically by the private sector,
  so the priority for public policy is to eliminate any remaining policy
  constraints on trade and markets and to invest in public goods that
  encourage private investments. By far the greatest policy challenge,
  when growth is driven by the private sector, is to find ways of including the poor.
- *Medium- to high-potential areas with limited market access,* especially in Africa, represent a major priority and challenge for the development community. Intensification and diversification are the two
  primary strategies for these areas. Both strategies are aided by better
  access to input and output markets, complemented by the development of effective systems to generate and disseminate technologies.
  Aside from investing in infrastructure and technology, the main entry
  points should be to support options for managing risk, the development of land markets, and improved land management to mitigate
  land degradation. It is critically important to sequence these interventions carefully, especially to get markets working.
- *Marginal drylands,* where some of the world's poorest people live,
  present especially difficult challenges. Moving out of agriculture is by

far the most important strategy for poverty reduction in these areas, followed by growth in off-farm employment. As leaving agriculture is generally a longer-term proposition, those agricultural systems that remain viable must be developed in the short and medium term to reduce poverty. The main hurdle for marginal areas (and their often minority populations) is to involve them in the policy dialogue and to design safety nets that do not encourage dependency or crowd out local private initiatives. A new generation of agropastoral projects, implemented by many partners with the World Bank, is showing much promise in building on community management, risk management, and access to markets in these difficult environments.

Getting Agriculture Back onto the Development Agenda

Much progress can be made toward the Millennium Development Goals if the international community takes concerted action in five key areas:

1. *Involve agricultural stakeholders more closely in policy and investment decisions.* Efforts to foster a strong presence of agricultural stakeholders in international and national processes to formulate policy and allocate resources would logically shift the priority in policy adjustment and investments in their favor. Better policy and investment decisions can also be made if agricultural policy makers interact more effectively with a wider array of stakeholders and if they have better access to information based on careful analytical work. More attention must be given to the quality and timeliness of analytical work, to the quality of stakeholders' involvement in this work, and to ensuring that the resulting information is made available at the right time and through the right channels for successful dialogue. More analysis and attention to the political economy surrounding decision making on policy and investment priorities are also needed.
2. *Tailor agricultural investment needs more closely to financial instruments.* Currently investments in agriculture are financed mostly through the more conventional sector investment instruments. A more diversified approach, which takes advantage of the full array of financial instruments for agricultural investment, exploiting their complementarity and synergy, is required. Different financing instruments are needed (and used) as a particular innovation moves from experimentation to piloting, implementation, dissemination of good practice, and finally to wider scaling up and adoption. The World Bank, along with other donors, is shifting its emphasis from supporting discrete projects to providing programmatic funding, which offers direct budgetary support to implement an agreed-upon expenditure program. A comprehensive development

program requires programmatic lending to be combined with investment lending.

3. *Reduce processing costs for agricultural projects, especially by ensuring that good practice is scaled up.* Agricultural investment projects are more costly to prepare, partly because a higher number of environmental and social safeguards must be in place. Current trends to move the safeguard assessment from the project to the national level, and to rely more on national capabilities to reduce costs, should continue. By scaling up when appropriate and increasing the number of beneficiaries, it is also possible to reduce preparation and investment costs per beneficiary.

4. *Identify innovative channels to support direct investments in agriculture, in particular through public-private partnerships and greater involvement of the private sector.* Innovative ways to channel investment funds to agriculture are being identified, such as the use of matching grants and closer work with the private sector, as described earlier.

5. *Maintain the successful program to enhance the quality of World Bank lending, and share what has been learned with other donors and sources of funding.* The quality of agricultural operations funded by the World Bank, as determined by end-of-project reviews by the Operations Evaluation Department, has improved significantly in recent years. However, more can be done to improve the impact of agricultural investments on poverty and to document that impact through simpler but more relevant monitoring and evaluation systems. A final challenge is to learn more from development partners about emerging good practice and innovations. The Global Donor Platform for Rural Development has been established for this purpose.

Encouraging Developments

The recent upturn in the volume and quality of financial support for agricultural development is encouraging. It appears to result from (1) a greater awareness of the significant contribution that broad-based agricultural growth can make to reducing poverty and hunger and sustaining the environment in low-income countries, (2) the increase in national and local ownership of policies and investments, and (3) the much broader and more flexible range of financial instruments and development tools now available to support agriculture.

Against this background, the general picture with regard to practical knowledge for agricultural development is also encouraging. Much experience is now available on the kinds of investments needed to strengthen physical, human, social, and natural capital in the developing world. Issues that merit further study or piloting include (1) the major factors that determine whether key aspects of economic sector work are integrated into the policy and investment discussion, (2) the major factors that determine whether all stakeholders participate in this discussion, (3) tools for designing investments that reduce poverty efficiently through agriculture, and (4) the instruments and incentives required to develop more efficient partnerships between the public and private sectors to meet core requirements for agricultural growth that benefits the poor, including financial services, market development, and risk management.

Finally, the agricultural sector can command greater attention by clearly communicating the impact of agricultural investments on economic growth and the welfare of the poor. By improving the monitoring and evaluation of agricultural investments, it is possible to understand the magnitude of their impacts and to improve future investments. By sharing this information more widely, the development community will increase the likelihood that more and better investments are made in agriculture, that the world comes closer to attaining the MDGs, and that public awareness of agriculture's contributions to achieving the MDGs improves.

1

The Role of Agricultural Growth in Development Strategies to Benefit the Poor

In this chapter

Growth in agriculture will contribute directly to achieving four of the Millennium Development Goals (MDGs): (1) halving the proportion of people living in extreme poverty and hunger, (2) promoting gender equality and empowering women, (3) ensuring environmental sustainability, and (4) developing global partnerships through increased market access. Indirectly, agricultural growth will contribute to achieving several other MDGs.

Agricultural growth contributes to the MDGs through many paths, described in detail in this chapter. For example, agricultural growth can improve people's access to more and better-quality food; raise farm incomes; create employment on and off of the farm; and empower poor and marginalized groups, including women. It can also promote the sustainable management of natural resources.

In parts of the world (especially in Asia, through the green revolution), agricultural growth has a proven record of reducing poverty, hunger, and environmental problems. Agricultural growth has yet to make similar large strides in other parts of the world, but its remains fundamental to development in low-income countries (especially in Sub-Saharan Africa).

The contribution of agriculture will depend on the specific context, however. Agriculture will contribute in different ways to countries that are at different stages of development and that practice different types of agriculture. Four initial conditions improve the prospects for agriculture to bring about pro-poor growth: (1) the importance of agriculture to the poor, (2) the agroclimatic potential for improving productivity, (3) a reasonably equitable distribution of land, and (4) the importance of non-traded food staples to the poor.

The impact of agriculture[1] extends well beyond providing food security and higher incomes. Agricultural growth has spurred overall economic growth and successfully reduced poverty in settings as diverse as Chile, Ghana, India, Thailand, and Vietnam. As this chapter will show, this kind of sustained, rapid growth is essential if the world is to meet the Millennium Development Goals (MDGs) in the coming decade. The MDGs consist of specific global development targets that the international community seeks to reach by 2015 (box 1.1).

Institutions committed to achieving the MDGs, including the World Bank, must work from a deeper understanding of how agricultural growth contributes to each goal. They need a clear idea of the main entry points for catalyzing this growth, the specific structural changes that must be implemented, and the knowledge that academics and development specialists have accumulated on alternative approaches for achieving economic growth and equity in developing countries. This chapter highlights the specific ways in which agricultural growth will influence progress toward the poverty, hunger, gender, and environmental MDGs, and it discusses how agriculture's contributions to achieving the MDGs change according to each country's stage of growth.

Box 1.1 Millennium Development Goals, 1990–2015

Goals to which agriculture can make major direct contributions are indicated in boldface.

1. **Eradicate extreme poverty and hunger**
   - **Halve the proportion of people with less than US$1 a day**
   - **Halve the proportion of people who suffer from hunger**
2. Achieve universal primary education
3. **Promote gender equality and empower women**
4. Reduce child mortality
5. Improve maternal health
6. Combat HIV/AIDS, malaria, and other diseases
7. **Ensure environmental sustainability**
   - **Integrate sustainable development into country policies and reverse loss of environmental resources**
8. **Develop a global partnership for development, including market access**
   - **Reduce average tariffs on agricultural products**
   - **Reduce domestic and export agricultural subsidies in OECD countries**

Source: www.developmentgoals.org.

Agriculture's Central Role in Meeting the Millennium Development Goals

Four of the MDGs relate directly to the agricultural sector: halving the proportion of people living in extreme poverty and hunger, promoting gender equality and empowering women, ensuring environmental sustainability, and developing global partnerships through increased market access. The remaining MDGs have important indirect links to agricultural growth. For instance, access to better-quality food will improve health and reduce disease susceptibility, especially in women and children; and additional income from higher agricultural productivity will increase household investments in children's education.[2] The sections that follow explore agriculture's direct and indirect links with the MDGs in greater detail.

Agriculture Is Integral to Reducing Poverty

To halve the global population who survive on less than US$1 a day by 2015, the development community requires a multifaceted strategy that strongly supports agricultural growth that benefits the poor. In low-income countries, broad-based growth in agricultural productivity is one of the most effective ways of reducing poverty because it increases the incomes of small-scale farmers; raises the wages earned by landless laborers; and improves the availability, quality, and accessibility of food. Rapid increases in agricultural productivity in areas benefiting from the green revolution, for example, were accompanied by sharp increases in the incomes of poor households. Contrary to popular opinion, the benefits were often larger for landless laborers and small-scale farmers than for large-scale farmers (figure 1.1).

Aside from these direct benefits, increased agricultural productivity also brings strong indirect benefits to the poor by reducing food prices and creating jobs. Poor households, rural as well as urban, spend a large percentage of their income on food staples. Increased productivity of staple crops makes them less expensive. For example, cassava is the most important food staple in Nigeria; when research institutes[3] introduced improved cassava varieties in Nigeria in the 1980s, yields rose about 30 percent. Consumers captured an estimated 72 percent of the benefits of cassava research through lower prices, and poorer consumers, including poor farmers, captured a disproportionately high share of these benefits (figure 1.2).

Increased agricultural production and value-added processing are often labor-intensive enterprises that create jobs for the poor both on and off the farm. As agricultural production grows, agricultural employment typically

**Figure 1.1 Changes in Household Incomes in Southern India,
1973–84**

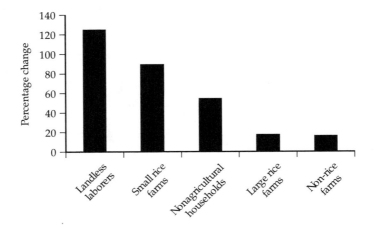

Source: Hazell and Ramasamy 1991.

grows by 0.3 to 0.6 percent, and employment outside of agriculture grows
by around 0.9 percent (Mellor 2001). Estimates of the extent to which
poverty falls as agricultural productivity rises are therefore generally high.
For example, a 1 percent increase in crop yield reduces the number of poor
people by 0.72 percent in Africa and by 0.48 percent in Asia (table 1.1). In

**Figure 1.2 Impact of Cassava R&D on Household Income
in Nigeria**

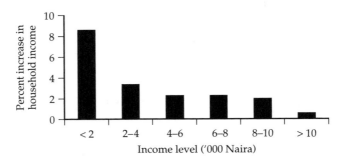

Source: Afolami and Falusi 1999.

Table 1.1 Effect of 1 Percent Increase in Crop Yields on Poverty Reduction

Region	Percent in poverty	Number in poverty (millions)	Percent reduction in number of poor in relation to a 1 percent yield increase
East Asia	15	278	0.48
South Asia	40	522	0.48
Africa	46	291	0.72
Latin America	16	78	0.10

Source: Thirtle, Lin, and Piesse 2003.

India, this effect on poverty reduction has been estimated at 0.4 percent in the short run and 1.9 percent in the long run, the latter through the indirect effects of lower food prices and higher wages (figure 1.3).

As one would expect, the contributions of agricultural growth to reducing poverty are quite specific to the local context. Agricultural growth has had a substantial, broad-based impact on poverty reduction where the following conditions are in place:

- Agriculture is important to the incomes of the rural poor.
- Climate and soils allow significant potential for productivity and profitability to grow.
- Land distribution is relatively equitable.

Figure 1.3 India: Elasticity of Poverty Reduction with Respect to Yield Growth, 1958–94

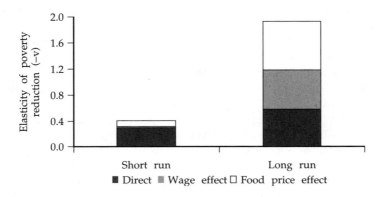

Source: Datt and Ravallion 1998.

- The poor consume nontraded food staples. Even cereals in many parts of Africa are essentially nontraded goods, because the lack of roads leads to high transport costs, which serve as a barrier to trade flows.

If agriculture is to help reduce poverty in areas where most of these conditions are not in place, agricultural growth must be targeted specifically to the commodities and agro-ecological regions that are important to the poor. In areas where agriculture's importance to the rural poor is declining, an increasing share of household income comes from remittances and from income earned off of the farm. There agriculture cannot contribute as much to reducing poverty as in other contexts. In areas where agriculture remains important but the distribution of assets, especially land, is extremely inequitable, overall growth in agriculture may contribute little to reducing poverty. For example, in Latin America, where land ownership is highly unequal, a 1 percent increase in yields is estimated to reduce the number of poor by only 0.1 percent (table 1.1). On the other hand, in Sub-Saharan Africa, rapid growth in a large number of areas with the conditions for broad-based agricultural growth could make an enormous contribution to the MDG of reducing poverty.

Agriculture Is Integral to Reducing Hunger and Malnutrition

Food security is achieved when people have access to sufficient food for a healthy and active life. The world still has 800 million food-insecure or hungry people, including 150 million children. Today there is more than enough food to feed everyone, but many households still lack the economic resources to produce or purchase sufficient food. The two indicators for progress toward the MDG on reducing hunger are the percentage of underweight children under five years of age and the percentage of people who are undernourished. Despite impressive gains in improving energy intake, about 25 percent of children less than five years of age in developing countries are underweight.[4] Large differences remain across countries and regions. Six percent of children under five are underweight in Latin America, for example, compared with 28 percent in Asia. Asia has the greatest number of chronically undernourished people—particularly India (214 million) and China (135 million)—followed by Africa (198 million). Africa is the only region where indicators for underweight children and undernourishment are worsening.

Most of the world's hungry and malnourished people are the rural poor, who do not produce enough food to meet household needs. Half of the world's hungry people are smallholder farmers; landless rural people add another one fifth; and pastoralists, fishers, and people whose livelihoods depend on forests make up one tenth.[5] These people are especially vulnerable to volatile food prices, which result from climate- and pest-induced fluctuations in food production, and to poor infrastructure, which limits access to food and input markets. During sustained food shortages, people are often forced to consume capital assets, such as breeding livestock and seed, which they would otherwise invest in future production. Insufficient food and poor diets deplete people's energy and immunity to disease, reduce their labor productivity and income, and deepen the cycle of poverty and hunger.

As farmers and mothers, women play a critical role in family food security, which makes the nutritional status of women a particularly important concern. Confronted with dwindling household food supplies, women often sacrifice their own nutritional well-being for that of others. For example, for every 10 percent drop in average rainfall compared with the long-term average in Zimbabwe, women's body mass index fell by 1.15 percent while men were unaffected (Quisumbing 2003).

Agriculture improves food security in many ways, most fundamentally by increasing the amount of food but also by providing the means to purchase food. Introducing new crop and livestock products and varieties (e.g., varieties that contain more nutrients or that mature more rapidly to mitigate seasonal hunger) can help ensure that more of the dietary needs of the poor are met and that seasonal food shortages are not as chronic as they were previously. Through growth in agricultural productivity and higher farm profits, the rural poor can generate additional income to purchase more food, including more diverse kinds of food. Some poverty reduction strategies recognize the importance of satisfying the immediate need for food before addressing longer term development goals. For example, the "twin-track" approach to reducing poverty used by the Food and Agriculture Organization (FAO) combines agricultural and rural development to create opportunities for poor people to improve their livelihoods, while meeting the immediate food and nutritional needs of seriously undernourished groups[6] so that they can increase their physical capacity to work.

Unless more attention is given to promoting agricultural growth, debilitating hunger will persist. According to the International Food Policy Research Institute (IFPRI), without a renewed commitment to agriculture through greater public and private investment and complementary policies, the long-term trend of falling food prices will not be maintained to 2020, and the opportunity to achieve hunger-related MDG targets will be compromised (World Bank 2005b) (figure 1.4). The IFPRI projections show that child malnutrition will decline by only 21 percent worldwide under a business-as-usual[7] baseline scenario, but a concerted effort (the "optimistic scenario") to improve policies and increase investments in agriculture could reduce child malnutrition by an estimated 43 percent between now and 2020—closer to the MDG target of 50 percent.

Figure 1.4 Malnourished Children in 2020: Alternative Scenarios by Region

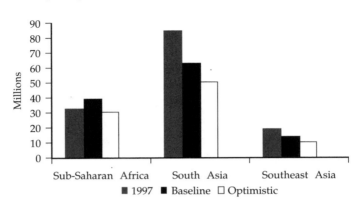

Source: Rosegrant et al. 2001.

Agriculture Promotes Gender Equality and Empowers Women

The third MDG aims to promote gender equality and empower women. Nearly half of the world's farmers are women. Women often provide the largest share of agricultural labor, especially where the incidence of poverty and hunger is high, as in Sub-Saharan Africa (figure 1.5). As more men pursue employment off of the farm, women assume a more critical role in rural areas. Approximately one third of the rural households in Sub-Saharan Africa are headed by women, whose burden is often made all the heavier by the prevalence of HIV/AIDS.

In addition to income poverty, many rural women experience "time poverty," which reduces their ability to produce food (thus further increasing food insecurity), limits their capacity to participate in income-generating activities (reducing household income), and constrains their capacity to save and invest (increasing household vulnerability). Heavy workloads can also induce women to remove their children from school.

Improvements to agriculture alone will not be sufficient to meet the goals of the "gender MDG"; a multisectoral approach is fundamental. Women's burden of work will be considerably eased by investments in water supplies and fuel sources. Women will benefit from opportunities in agriculture that help them to use their special skills for remunerative purposes, such as skills in small livestock production, horticulture, or processing and packaging.

Figure 1.5 Rural Workload by Gender: Selected African Countries

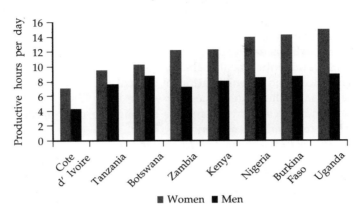

Source: Brown and Haddad, 1995; Saito, 1992.

Agricultural policies can be adjusted to support the needs of women farmers. In Kenya, for example, gender equality in access to farm inputs could
increase output by 20 percent or more (Blackden and Banu 1999).

Choices in Agriculture Can Restore the Environment

Choices made with respect to agriculture in the coming years will determine whether agriculture's extensive influence on the environment is
positive or negative. Agriculture is by far the largest user of land and
water resources, accounting for 86 percent of water consumption in
developing countries in 1995 (Rosegrant, Cai, and Cline 2002) and 34
percent of total land area in 2000 (FAOSTAT 2003). Agricultural production directly affects soil and water quality, the level of biodiversity, the
aesthetic appearance of the landscape, and global changes in the environment.

*Several agricultural approaches can bring the world closer to the specific land,
water, forest, and global climate change targets[8] of the MDG for environmental
sustainability. These approaches must*

- *Intensify agriculture in a sustainable manner:* Sustainable intensification of agriculture is critical to the seventh target of the environment
  MDG, which is to integrate principles of sustainable development into
  national policies and programs and reverse the loss of environmental
  resources. More than 1.9 billion hectares of land (a billion is 1,000 million),

mostly in developing countries, have soils that have been degraded through human activity (FAO 2003b). Large-scale degradation of agricultural land occurs chiefly because of erosion, soil nutrient mining (particularly in Africa), nutrient overload, indiscriminate use of pesticides, and salinization caused by irrigation schemes. A further environmental and public health challenge is posed by the rapid growth, concentration, and intensification of animal production and aquaculture, especially the management of waste from these systems. Policy changes and investments to induce sustainable management will be critical for reversing these trends.

- *Pursue integrated approaches to water use:* Although irrigated agriculture will continue to be the major user of water resources, competition from other sectors (e.g., industry, environmental conservation, and domestic use) is increasing. Improving the efficiency of current water resources through integrated approaches is far preferable than attempting to expand water supplies. Without integrated approaches to improving how water is allocated and used, the MDG target of halving the proportion of people without sustainable access to safe drinking water will not be met by 2015.

- *Reduce deforestation:* Over the past four decades, the total forested area, including new forest used for commercial purposes, has shrunk by 5 percent while agricultural area has expanded by more than 10 percent. The need or incentive to clear land for agriculture is lessened by making the world's current crop and pasture land more productive. Forestry can be incorporated into small-scale crop and livestock farming in many ways, including agroforestry, plantations for industrial use, and environmental services such as carbon sequestration and shade-grown produce. All of these approaches improve farmers' incomes while meeting the MDG target of increasing the land area dedicated to forest resources.

- *Reduce greenhouse gas emissions:* Agriculture is one of the largest contributors to the emission of greenhouse gasses. These gases are emitted by burning fossil fuels and biomass from deforestation, by ruminant digestion and rice fields (about 20 times more aggressive than carbon dioxide in global warming), and by nitrous oxide produced mostly from storing manure and overusing fertilizer (about 200 times more aggressive than carbon dioxide). Investments in sustainable agricultural systems such as conservation tillage, improved livestock nutrition, and manure management will contribute directly to the MDGs for improving energy efficiency and reducing greenhouse gas emissions. Agriculture can also reduce greenhouse gases by serving as a carbon sink, and in some areas summer pastures are being used for "carbon farming."

*Realizing Agriculture's Potential Contributions
to the Millennium Development Goals: Three Main
Entry Points for the World Bank*

The World Bank and other donors now focus much of their support on
policies and investments aimed at reducing poverty and achieving other
MDGs. For agriculture, the World Bank has a comparative advantage in
working through three main entry points for achieving these goals:

- *Raising global awareness of agriculture's role in reducing poverty:*
  World Bank senior management has effectively raised global awareness of such issues as environmental degradation, water, and education. A similar effort for agriculture would contribute significantly to
  strategies for reducing poverty. The World Bank has the power to bring
  together the many groups with an interest in supporting agricultural
  development to benefit the poor. The Global Donor Platform for Rural
  Development, in which the World Bank is an active member (see chapter 6), is one important channel for creating and enhancing global
  awareness about agriculture and poverty.
- *Focusing analysis on agriculture's potential as an engine of growth:*
  This entry point is particularly important for those low-income countries where agriculture is important to the poor, the resource base offers
  potential for growth in productivity, land is distributed relatively equitably, and the poor consume a large proportion of nontraded staples.
  Representing a broad range of expertise in economic and social development, the World Bank can help identify major policies and investments that these countries can use to promote agriculture as a strong
  catalyst for overall economic development (box 1.2).
- *Promoting multisectoral approaches:* Although most MDGs, such as
  those related to gender, water, and hunger, cannot be achieved by
  working in one sector alone, they have often been neglected in development activities because no single sector, agriculture included, takes
  responsibility. With its multisectoral base, the World Bank can identify
  broad-based strategies for progress on these cross-cutting issues,
  although here the main challenge is to work collaboratively rather than
  competitively across sectors.

As Economies Change, Links between
Agriculture and the Poor Change

*Agriculture's contribution to achieving the MDGs for each country will
depend on that country's stage of growth.* In some countries, mostly in Africa,

---

Box 1.2 Tanzania: Agriculture as a Leader of Growth in the Early Stages of Development

In developing its agricultural strategy, the Government of Tanzania needed to discern whether its agricultural sector could serve as an engine of growth and poverty reduction or as a follower in an economy where growth was driven by other sectors. To be a leader, a sector must hold some comparative advantage and also have strong links to the rest of the economy. Comparative advantage analysis revealed that Tanzanian agriculture could be globally competitive in many food and commercial export crops. Despite a weak agribusiness sector, growth in agricultural income in Tanzania will have substantial effects on demand for consumer goods and services. In other words, agriculture's role in the Tanzanian economy is that of an engine of growth in the early stages of transformation.

Source: World Bank 2000.

---

agriculture is the dominant sector and must take a leading role in growth (table 1.2). For many other countries, however, agricultural growth—and opportunities for meeting the MDGs—will be fostered largely through growth in the nonfarm economy and in agricultural exports that can expand the market for agricultural products.

There is no universal pathway to development, but a stylized picture of structural transformation looks like this:

- *The least-developed economies are largely agrarian, and agriculture accounts for the largest share of employment, GDP, and export earnings.* Incomes are typically low, and most of the poor are farmers or laborers who depend on agriculture. Structural transformation begins when agricultural production is intensified through investments in land quality (e.g., irrigation), new agricultural technologies, market infrastructure, and new institutions to operate in the agriculture sector. In densely populated areas throughout the developing world, land-saving technologies, especially high-yielding varieties of food staples, have successfully catalyzed this transformation. The resulting production increases helped to raise farm income, reduce food prices, and spur increased demand for nonagricultural goods and services.

This early stage of transformation emphasizes broad-based agricultural growth because of agriculture's comparative advantage among all sectors of an economy and its strong links to growth in other sectors, aside from its direct effects on poverty. Where agricultural growth has

Table 1.2 The Share of Agriculture and Poor People in Developing and Transitional Countries

Country	Employment in agriculture (percent of total) 1995[a]	Agriculture, value added (percent of GDP) 2001[a]	Number living in US$2/day poverty (million) 2000[a]	Number living in US$1/day poverty (million) 2000[a]	Percent living in poverty (less than US$1/day) 2000[a]
East and Southeast Asia	49	14	873	261	15
Europe and Central Asia	25	10	101	20	4
Latin America	19	7	176	56	11
Middle East and North Africa	37[b]	11	32	8	3
South Asia	65	24	1052	432	32
Sub-Saharan Africa (excluding South Africa)	68[b]	27	504	323	49
All low- and middle-income countries	**46**	**12**	**2,138**	**896**	**22**

Sources: SIMA; World Bank 2003a, 2003c.
Note: The US$1 and US$2 per day poverty lines refer to $1.08 and $2.15 per day at 1993 PPP.
a. Data are for the years available for each variable.
b. 1990 figures.

Figure 1.6 Structural Transformation: Sub-Saharan Africa, 1961–2000

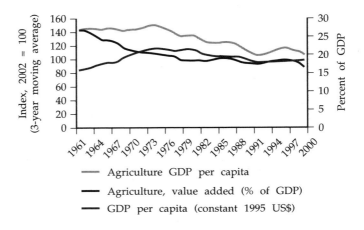

Source: World Bank 2003a.

stalled, as in Africa, overall economic growth and the structural transformation away from agriculture have also stalled (figure 1.6).

- *Over time, a modernizing agricultural sector creates jobs and off-farm income in agricultural processing and marketing, input supply and services, and related industries* (figure 1.7). Agribusiness enterprises are generally small and labor intensive, and they provide employment and incomes to local people. In India, for instance, agro-based enterprises accounted for 22 million of the 33 million workers in the manufacturing sector in the early 1990s (Chadha and Gulati 2002). Even when effects on agribusiness are modest, growth in farm income stimulates growth in other sectors by increasing the demand for consumer goods. Income growth stimulates demand for diversified, higher value products, especially horticultural and livestock products, which are generally also labor intensive to produce. Income growth can improve the quality of diets and labor productivity for agricultural and nonagricultural workers. A recent analysis indicates that when these growth links are taken into account, agriculture's contribution to GDP in Latin America is about 50 percent higher than official statistical estimates (de Ferranti et al. 2005).

In this stage of transformation, the share of income spent on food in aggregate declines (Engel's Law), as does agriculture's share of the economy (figure 1.8). Under these conditions, the market for agricultural

Figure 1.7 Agriculture and Agribusiness in Developing Countries: 1992

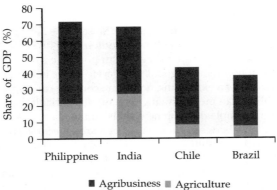

■ Agribusiness ■ Agriculture

Source: Pryor and Holt 1999.

Figure 1.8 Structural Transformation: East Asia and Pacific, 1961–2001

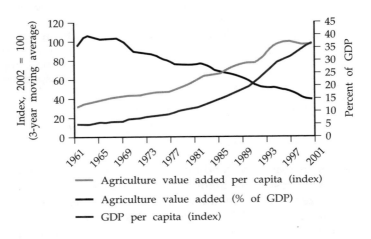

— Agriculture value added per capita (index)

— Agriculture value added (% of GDP)

— GDP per capita (index)

Source: World Bank 2003a.

Box 1.3 Links among Agriculture,
Rural Nonfarm Growth, and Urban Areas
Change as Economies Develop

In the early stages of development, the costs of transactions between rural and urban areas are high. Many agricultural goods simply do not get to the market, so growth in agriculture primarily supports the rural nonfarm economy, especially in nontradable goods and services (see inset table for examples). In rural areas, an expanding nonfarm economy can support agriculture by enabling it to meet growing demand for agricultural products and helping rural people develop new skills and contacts. As development progresses, links between rural and urban areas become stronger. Increased purchasing power shifts consumers' preferences to modern and tradable products, which are often more competitive than rural manufactures. At a later stage in the transformation, urban congestion and associated factors may induce some small-scale industry to move to rural areas where resources are cheaper.

Links Between Rural Nonfarm Economic Activities and Agricultural Growth, by Sector

Link to agriculture	Tradables	Nontradables
Production: forward	Processing and packaging of agricultural products	Marketing, transportation, and trade of agricultural products
Production: backward	Agricultural tools and equipment; input supply	Agricultural services (machinery repairs, veterinary services)
Consumption	Consumer goods	Home improvements, domestic services, construction, trade, and transportation

Source: Start 2001.

products is increasingly conditioned by urban demand and trade, especially with respect to higher value products. Within agriculture, commercialized farming—with its high share of marketed output and product quality defined by market signals rather than farm households' consumption preferences—expands, and production becomes more diversified.

- *As the profitability of agriculture relative to other activities decreases, and as nonagricultural activities account for a larger share of value-added in the economy, labor tends to be drawn out of the farm sector to capture higher wages* (box 1.3 on previous page). The share of the workforce in agriculture will nevertheless remain higher than the share of national income spent on agriculture, because of the costs of seeking and adapting to new employment and leaving the land. As a result, the incidence of poverty in rural areas will remain relatively high if these areas are neglected by investment and safety nets. Policies to help people leave the farm sector become crucial and raise new challenges for poverty reduction.
- *The final stages of the transformation occur when economic growth and rapidly rising wages for unskilled labor in the nonfarm sector draw labor out of agriculture.* The absolute number of workers in the sector falls sharply (figure 1.9), and farm consolidation allows those remaining to increase their income. Rural household incomes continue to diversify with increasing participation in the expanding rural nonfarm labor market, narrowing the income gap between rural and urban households (Gardner 2002).

The development of a concrete agricultural strategy to complement this stage of transformation is complicated by the fact that most economies consist of mixtures of these stages of development and diverse agricultural systems. It is also complicated by the diverse nature of the agricultural poor within and between countries (box 1.4). The chapters

Figure 1.9 The Percent and Number of People Employed in Agriculture, Poland and Brazil, 1962–1997

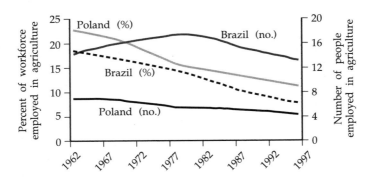

Source: World Bank 2003a.

Box 1.4 Who and Where Are the "Agricultural Poor"?

About 70 percent of the world's poor live in rural areas, and of these, a large majority depend directly on agriculture for part of their livelihoods. These agricultural poor are highly diverse. Most are small-scale farmers, herders, and fishers who earn anywhere from 20 to 80 percent of their income from agriculture, both from their own farms and from working for other farmers. In some regions, such as South Asia, some of the poorest are landless laborers who depend on agriculture for much of their work. In many regions, particular groups are disproportionately represented in the agricultural poor, especially indigenous groups, female-headed households, and the aged. For most of the agricultural poor, earnings from nonfarm work, migration, and remittances are increasingly important. Secure access to assets (especially good land) and to markets will often determine who is and is not poor. The poor are often concentrated in areas where land and other natural resources are poor, or where settlements are remote and inaccessible. Although the poorest groups are often located in areas that are marginal because of their poor natural resources and remoteness, the absolute number of poor may be higher in regions with better natural resources but with weak infrastructure or poor governance. In rapidly developing countries, however, the poor generally tend to become concentrated in less-favored areas.

Vulnerability to natural shocks (especially drought) and human-induced disasters (especially conflict) is endemic among the agricultural poor. When conditions improve, poor people can move out of poverty for a time, but repeated shocks often condemn people to suffer chronic poverty over a long period.

Poverty is not merely a lack of resources. Poor people lack political power—locally, nationally, and globally. Excluded from the debates that could improve their circumstances, the agricultural poor have suffered from decades of urban favoritism in development strategies. The rural poor have experienced much discrimination, even compared with the urban poor, in access to such basic services as water, health, sanitation, and education. The poor in more remote and sparsely populated areas, and disenfranchised groups such as women and indigenous people, are especially deprived of these services.

These various dimensions of poverty are highlighted in the strategies proposed in this report, and special attention is given to their diverse circumstances in the discussion of agricultural megasystems in chapter 5. The strategies reflect a three-pronged approach to poverty reduction—increasing economic opportunity, facilitating empowerment, and reducing vulnerability.

Sources: IFAD 2004; Kelly and Byerlee 2003; World Bank 2001.

that follow will provide much of the detail needed to understand the true dimensions of this challenge and the wealth of approaches available to meet it. Chapter 2 will begin by taking a closer look at the forces that are bringing about profound change in agriculture and that must be taken into account when making decisions about agricultural strategies, policies, institutions, and investments.

2
The Rapidly Changing Context for Agriculture: Challenges and Opportunities

In this chapter

Changing global forces will strongly influence economic growth, poverty, and the supply of agricultural commodities:

- *Changing market conditions:* From the local to the global level, markets and demand for agricultural commodities are changing rapidly, especially for higher value products such as horticultural crops and other niche products. For developing countries, these changes constitute an opportunity to diversify their agriculture and exploit their advantage in providing labor-intensive products. They also constitute a growing challenge, especially to small-scale farmers, to deliver products that meet stringent standards and to coordinate their activities more effectively.
- *Climate change and natural resource degradation:* Widespread environmental change is altering agricultural potential throughout the world. Producers will require new knowledge and technology to cope adequately with the challenges and opportunities that arise.
- *Demography and health:* As more people migrate to urban areas in search of employment, the rural population will decline in some regions and become older, and women will play an even more prominent role in agriculture. The composition of rural households will also change considerably as a consequence of HIV/AIDS.
- *Agricultural science and technology:* Advances in agricultural knowledge and technology can create an array of new choices for producers, altering what is produced, where it is produced, and how it is produced. Promising prospects for solving food and agricultural problems may elude developing countries and poor farmers if they fail to access the new knowledge and technology developed by the private sector.
- *Stakeholders' changing roles and interests:* The private sector and markets will drive agricultural growth. The public sector must work more closely with the private sector, nongovernmental organizations

(box continued next page)

(box continued)

(NGOs), civil society, and international donor and finance organizations to develop novel approaches that enable agriculture to benefit
from new knowledge and technologies, facilitate competition in
markets, and compensate for growing scarcities of natural resources.

Success in agricultural development has been based largely on increasing
the use of land, irrigation, and inputs to expand production of staple
grains and a small range of export commodities, but these strategies must
be sharply adjusted to accommodate new realities. Changing market conditions and supply chains increasingly influence agricultural production.
They also define the conditions that allow farm households, especially
those of small-scale farmers, to participate in markets. Climatic risk, a
depleted natural resource base, and a changing labor force are also profoundly altering the developing world's rural areas.

This chapter highlights the opportunities as well as the challenges that
these and other trends present for agricultural growth and poverty reduction. The discussion looks at agricultural change from several perspectives, taking into account factors that influence supply and demand; the
expanding international web of regulations concerning agricultural products and trade; global trends that are transforming the biophysical and
socioeconomic environment of agriculture; and the growing number of
organizations and institutions that have an interest in the fate of the agricultural sector.

The Changing Context: The Demand Side

Food and agricultural systems must repond to rapidly changing market
conditions. These include both global and domestic markets, and both
product composition as well as product quality.

Commodity Markets Are Changing Dramatically

World markets for agricultural products from developing countries
have changed profoundly in recent decades. Commodities traditionally
exported by developing countries, such as coffee and cotton, have experienced unprecedented low prices (figure 2.1). Despite rapidly growing

Figure 2.1 Real Commodity Prices, 1975–2001

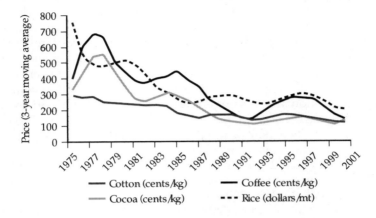

Source: IMF International Financial Statistics.

demand for higher value products (figure 2.2), the overall trade balance for agricultural products has worsened. Developing countries historically have had a net surplus in agricultural trade, but this surplus declined steadily over the past four decades as imports grew faster than exports, largely because of deteriorating terms of trade.

Figure 2.2 Changing Composition of Developing Country Agro-Food Exports

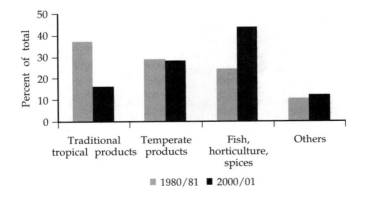

Source: World Bank 2005c.

Many developing countries still depend on a narrow range of traditional commodities for export. This dependence, aggravated by unreliable levels of production and quality and volatile international markets, has brought many farm households to a crisis, worsening poverty and vulnerability throughout rural areas. Low commodity prices largely reflect slow growth in demand for those commodities, foreshadowing a long-term decline in world prices. A good example is the "coffee crisis" that occurred when developing countries increased production while per capita consumption in importing countries stagnated. Coffee prices on the international market began a precipitous slide in late 2000, falling to less than one-third of their 1997 peak by the end of 2001. The consequences for farmers, laborers, and even some national economies have been devastating. Prices are expected to recover somewhat over the next decade but are unlikely to return to the highs of the 1970s and mid-1990s for any sustained period (World Bank 2003d).

At the global level, commodity prices have fallen partly because of agricultural subsidies and protectionist policies in industrialized countries. These subsidies and policies are particularly strong for commodities produced by developing as well as developed countries, such as sugar, meat, and cotton. At the national level, liberalization and privatization have left domestic producers and consumers far less insulated from global price fluctuations. Fluctuating exchange rates, climatic variability, and poor infrastructure have further heightened the uncertainty of farm incomes that rely on export commodities.

It is important to emphasize that market prospects are not all bleak, however, even in the traditional commodity sector. Low-income countries that continue to experience rapid population growth will fuel growing demand for cereal crops for food, and real prices for grains in world markets are projected to remain stable after a prolonged period of decline (World Bank, 2005b). This trend will provide a significant market opportunity for the many low-income countries where a majority of poor farm households depend on cereals. For instance, a simulation analysis suggests that in Ethiopia the strongest contribution to growth that benefits the poor will come from improving productivity in cereals and other staple crops (World Bank 2005b).

The prospects for higher value agricultural products seem even more promising than prospects for traditional commodities. Income gains in many middle-income and transitional countries have caused a revolution in demand. Consumers are willing and able to purchase a more diversified consumption basket that includes a greater share of high-value products (figure 2.3). Income growth in the rapidly developing countries of East Asia has already inspired the dramatic increases in demand for animal products (Delgado et al. 1999). By 2020, the population of the developing

Figure 2.3 Per Capita Consumption Increase by Food Group, India, 1977–99

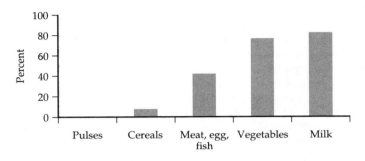

Source: Joshi et al. 2002.

world is expected to consume 55 percent more meat and 60 percent more milk than they do today. They will also demand more fish products, which cannot be supplied through marine and inland fisheries alone. Aquaculture will increasingly have to make up the deficit.

Export markets are expanding rapidly for fish and horticultural products, including tropical fruits, vegetables, organic products, and cut flowers (figure 2.2), and these growing markets are opening new opportunities for agriculture to function as an engine of growth and poverty reduction in many countries. Vegetables and fruits accounted for over 7 percent of developing country agricultural exports in 2001, and the total contribution comes to well over 10 percent when processed and partially transformed fruits and vegetables are included (FAO 2004b). Even in stagnant economies, such as Kenya, the horticulture sector experienced a growth of more than 200 percent between 1993 and 1998.

As exciting as prospects for new crops appear, growth that benefits poor people is usually best encouraged by supporting both traditional and nontraditional commodities. For example, simultaneous increases in exports in several countries aiming at the same markets can drive down world prices, posing a major risk for the latecomers. Price trends for avocados, green beans, green peas, mangoes, and pineapples demonstrate this risk (FAO 2004b). In addition, nontraditional products still constitute such a small share of the agricultural sector that they will have a limited impact on overall growth of the agricultural sector in the near term, even with rapid growth (box 2.1). A related concern is that an overemphasis on higher-value markets will crowd out investments in the traditional commodities on which most poor farmers continue to depend.

Box 2.1 Nontraditional Products in Uganda and Kenya

By definition, nontraditional export crops initially constitute a small share
of national exports, which limits the impact of early, rapid growth in nontraditional exports on overall agricultural performance. Contrasting experiences in Kenya and Uganda demonstrate this point. Kenya exported
4,000 tons of cut flowers and foliage in 1981, an amount that had increased
to 30,000 tons by 1998. In terms of value, cut flower exports rose from
US$86 million in 1994 to US$141 million in 2000, amounting to 10 percent
of Kenya's agricultural exports and 5.5 percent of agricultural value-
added production. In the late 1990s, Uganda started exporting cut flowers.
Although the value of Uganda's flower exports has tripled from US$3 mil-
lion to US$9.8 million, flowers still represent a small share of total exports
(only 2 percent of agricultural exports and 0.3 percent of agricultural value
added). The expansion of floriculture in Uganda has undoubtedly
improved the lives of many individuals, but it is unlikely to have a substantial effect on the overall performance of the agricultural sector for a
decade or more.

Sources: Diao, Dorosh, and Rathman 2003; FAO 2004b.

The Consumer Revolution: Demanding Safer Food

Agricultural and food products are now more frequently consumed far
from their places of origin, but the increased availability of these products
has heightened the risk that diseases caused by food-borne pathogens
will spread and that undesirable pesticide and chemical residues will con-
taminate food. Consumer concerns over food safety have become more
acute with the appearance of such problems as "mad cow" disease, *E. coli*
contamination of meat, *Cyclospora* in raspberries, and chemical contamination of olive oil. Many consumers are willing to pay a higher price for
foods that they perceive to be safer, such as organically grown products.

*Increased demand for safer and higher-quality food products is reflected by the
proliferating number of public and private sanitary and phytosanitary (SPS)
requirements for food products and processing.* The requirement for hazard
analysis and critical control points (HACCP)-based systems is becoming
a common feature of public food safety regulations in developed countries and covers imported as well as domestic food products. Importing
countries, wary of pests that could harm domestic agriculture, are also
requiring agricultural imports to meet a growing array of phytosanitary
standards. Consumers, retailers, governments, and civil society are
now all involved in designing and implementing standards for products

(e.g., quality, size, chemical residues, and level of microbial contamination) and their production processes (e.g., labor standards and environmental impacts).

The complexity and potential costs of meeting these standards pose challenges to small-scale farmers. They also create potential trade barriers for developing countries that lack the technical capacity to prove the safety and quality of their products. Chapter 3 will look at ways of addressing these issues.

The Changing Context: The Supply Side

The changing natural environment and labor force are negatively affecting agricultural potential throughout the world. However, even more rapid changes in agricultural technology have the potential to sharply accelerate agricultural growth.

Supply Chains: The Response to the Consumer Revolution

Systems for procuring and distributing food have been transformed by food safety concerns and the related expansion of domestic and global markets for higher-value products. Higher-value products present a range of technical challenges in production and processing. They also present numerous institutional challenges for coordinating activities along the market chain, meeting quality standards, and accessing market information. Domestic as well as export markets now focus on the entire food chain from "farm to fork."

Supermarkets, for example, were once on the fringes of food marketing in developing countries, but now they account for 45 to 75 percent of national food retail sales in six Latin American countries, 33 to 63 percent in Southeast and East Asia, and 55 percent in South Africa (Reardon, Timmer, and Berdegue 2003). These retailers are often multinational firms with highly centralized procurement and distribution systems. From their suppliers, they demand reliable flows of products of consistent quality, and they increasingly apply their own standards for quality, safety, traceability, and social values, such as prohibiting child labor and protecting animal welfare. Although supermarkets create opportunities for producers who can meet their standards, they also increase the risk that small-scale farmers will be excluded. For example, scattered groups of smallholders may find it quite difficult to meet traceability requirements intended to ensure consumer safety (Boselie, Henson, and Weatherspoon 2003). While such measures apply mainly to export products, there is growing evidence in middle-income developing countries of supermarkets' growing predominance in serving domestic consumers and employing stricter coordination and controls along the supply chain.

Contract farming is increasingly used to ensure a predictable supply of products that meets quality specifications. Under the terms of the contract, the farmer generally contributes land and labor, and the processor/retailer (the "integrator") provides the inputs, which often include working capital and technical assistance. The standardized inputs and technical assistance enable farmers to meet the food safety and quality control requirements imposed on higher value products. In many developing countries, however, smallholder producers sometimes still have no choice but to sell their products to a monopoly integrator, and so they risk losing profitability, independence, and market power.

The shift from bulk commodities to higher-value products has also broadened the basis of competitiveness. Competition is based not only on safety and quality but increasingly on branding, intellectual property, specialized competencies, and reputation with suppliers and customers. As a result, growth is concentrated in areas that have advantages in infrastructure, skilled managerial resources, and legal and regulatory institutions.

The overall equity effects of these trends for poor producers and consumers are complex. The "supermarket revolution," for example, may encourage more efficient domestic marketing and reduce food prices for the urban poor. The production and packaging of higher-value produce generate considerable employment for unskilled labor. The increasing importance of branding and product differentiation may provide opportunities for converting traditional export commodities (e.g., coffee) into differentiated and potentially more profitable products (e.g., shade grown, organically grown, or fair trade coffee). Organic certification, designations of origin, and certifications concerning labor practices or treatment of growers (fair trade) confer brand attributes and give small-scale farmers access to new, higher-value markets.

In conclusion, while prices for many traditional commodities will probably continue to decline over the long term, exciting opportunities are emerging in nontraditional products and in alternative product lines of traditional commodities. Opportunities for nontraditional products will change the way that production processes are organized, with international and domestic processors and retailers playing a more prominent role. While these trends might put pressure on the smallholder sector, they may have positive overall effects on equity by raising employment in nonfarm agribusiness and reducing food costs for the urban poor.

New Science, New Information Technology, and the Rural Poor

Agricultural growth now depends far more on expanding the application of scientific knowledge to farming than on expanding the amount of land, water, and

---

Box 2.2 Asia: Crop Yields Are Growing More Slowly

In Asia, cereal crop yields have grown more slowly in recent years than in the 1970s and 1980s because input use is already high and the costs of irrigation are rising. Other contributing factors include a slowing of investment in infrastructure and research (in part induced by declining commodity prices); a shift to more profitable, higher-quality but lower-yielding crop varieties; natural resource and environmental constraints; and poor policy environments. In some countries, more open trade regimes and low world cereal prices have made it more attractive to import grain than to increase local production.

Source: Authors.

---

external inputs dedicated to agriculture. Impressive gains in crop yields in developing countries in the 1970s and 1980s (especially gains achieved through the green revolution) generally were followed by slower agricultural growth in the 1990s. Growth in yields in developing countries dropped from 2.8 percent annually in the 1970s to 1.5 percent in the 1990s. This pattern has been especially evident in Asia (box 2.2), where many of the "easy gains" in agricultural productivity were made some time ago.

Because yield gains have such a significant impact on reducing poverty, however—a 1 percent increase in yields translates into a 0.5 to 0.8 percent decline in poverty—the need to sustain growth in yields is acute. How will this occur, especially if the easy gains have been made? Exponential progress in molecular biology and information technology promises to raise yields for farmers in developing countries and at the same time alter global patterns of competitive advantage. Although conventional crop breeding still offers considerable potential to raise yields, especially in neglected regions such as Sub-Saharan Africa, the tools of biotechnology—including genetic engineering—could help achieve such complex goals as enhancing the nutritional quality of staple food crops, reducing crop and livestock losses to pests and diseases, and stabilizing yields against drought and other climatic risks.

Whether biotechnology delivers on this promise, especially for poor people, remains to be seen. First, the environmental and food safety risks of genetically engineered foods continue to be debated. This debate deals with tradeoffs between risks on the one hand and poor people's needs for food security and food quality on the other. Second, the private sector generally controls the development and application of new tools and technologies in biotechnology (box 2.3). It focuses on crops and products of interest to commercial farmers, further widening the gap

---

Box 2.3 The Privatization of Knowledge for the Privileged Few

The dominance of private companies in agricultural R&D has important implications for poor people's access to new knowledge. Intellectual property rights (IPR) protection has led to a boom in R&D for biotechnology and information science, but IPR presents complex issues in accessing modern scientific tools and technologies for the benefit of the poor:

- *Access to new tools and products of biotechnology:* Most new tools and products of the biotechnology revolution are produced and patented by the private sector. The private sector has little commercial incentive to invest in technologies for small-scale farmers, while public research organizations require access to the new tools if they are to serve these farmers.
- *Patenting products of public research:* Public research organizations might need to seek proprietary protection of research findings to ensure that they remain available to the poor and to use as bargaining chips in acquiring proprietary technologies, especially new tools of biotechnology from the private sector.
- *Access to genetic resources:* Genetic resources have increased in potential value, but numerous questions are yet to be resolved regarding limitations on patenting genes, varieties, and livestock; ownership rights for traditional plant varieties; farmers' right to save seed; and indigenous knowledge.

Source: Authors.

---

with smallholders, many of whom produce "orphan crops" that are not widely commercialized. There is a legitimate role for the public sector in filling this gap, and for international donors such as the World Bank in supporting such a role.

Likewise, new information and communication technologies have the potential to revolutionize rural information systems, providing more and better information directly to farmers, extension agents, agribusinesses, and other service providers. *Despite their immense promise, these technologies are still far less available to the poor than to the rich, both within and across countries.* Further widening of the "digital divide" also results from illiteracy, remoteness, and relatively high initial and maintenance costs that put these new technologies beyond the reach of many smallholders. An emerging challenge in developing countries is to ensure that poor farmers, including women, can access these new technologies at affordable and competitive prices.

Natural Resources: Restoration or Deterioration?

Projections from the International Food Policy Research Institute indicate that agricultural production will need to increase in absolute volume by the same amount in the next 25 years as it has in the last 25 years (Rosegrant et al. 2001). The challenge is that few new land or water resources are available in most parts of the world, so they cannot be an important source of growth. Per capita land area for agricultural production declined from 0.30 to 0.16 hectares between 1961 and 2001 in developing countries. Supplies of water for agriculture are declining as competition from nonagricultural uses increases. In South Asia, the Middle East, and North Africa, water shortages have already reached critical levels for agriculture.

The natural resources needed to sustain agricultural production are not only increasingly scarce but increasingly degraded. Overgrazing, deforestation, soil loss, salinization, waterlogging, and the siltation of rivers and reservoirs are degrading land, water, and biodiversity. Waterlogged and saline soils threaten the productivity of many irrigated high-potential farming systems, including those that made dramatic productivity increases through the green revolution. For instance, resource degradation has offset much of the gain from investments in technology, infrastructure, and education in the Punjab of Pakistan (Ali and Byerlee 2002). Policy distortions, especially water pricing and a lack of research and extension on more sustainable cropping systems, have helped to set the stage for resource degradation. Of the nearly 1.5 billion hectares of cropland worldwide, it is estimated that 38 percent is degraded to some degree, with the highest proportion of degraded cropland found in Africa and Latin America (Scherr and Yadav 2001).

Although these figures are distressing, much of the damage to natural resources may still be reversed. Soil nutrient depletion, the most critical problem in many rainfed farming systems of Africa, can be addressed with soil amendments and appropriate farming systems. More generally, improved management practices can substantially increase the efficiency with which water and nutrients are used (box 2.4).

Given the limited scope to expand the use of natural resources in agricultural production, the main challenges will be to increase the efficiency with which productive resources are used and to promote sustainable natural resource management practices to meet changing demand patterns.

Migration, Health, and the Agricultural Labor Force

A number of major demographic changes pose important challenges for targeting support to the needs of specific rural populations. *Over the next 30 years, the rural population will remain relatively stable, whereas the urban*

Box 2.4 Conserving Resources for Agriculture

Throughout the world, significant inefficiencies exist in the ways land, water, and nutrients are used in agriculture; in protecting crops from losses after harvest; and in matching food needs with availability. No single action or technique can save resources on a large scale, but a combination of approaches can yield major, long-lasting gains. For example, although nearly universal compliance in applying fertilizer at the optimal time may save no more than 5 percent of all nitrogen, a combination of several measures (more careful timing of fertilizer application, appropriate placement of fertilizer, recycling crop residues, rotating crops including leguminous crops, and reducing tillage to minimize soil erosion) may bring a 20 to 30 percent gain in overall nitrogen recovery by crops. In many cases, producers could be induced to change their practices through reforms in the pricing systems that distort the actual costs of inputs.

Source: Smil 2004.

---

population in developing countries is expected to double (figures 2.4 and 2.5). The composition of rural populations will change as well. Rural residents will be older and more of them will be female, as young men leave agriculture to work in towns or in other countries (figure 2.6). This process is well underway in most regions of the world, especially in the former

Figure 2.4 Rural and Urban Population Growth in Asia, 2000–30

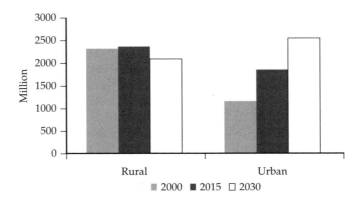

Figure 2.5 Share of Population in Urban Areas, 2000–30

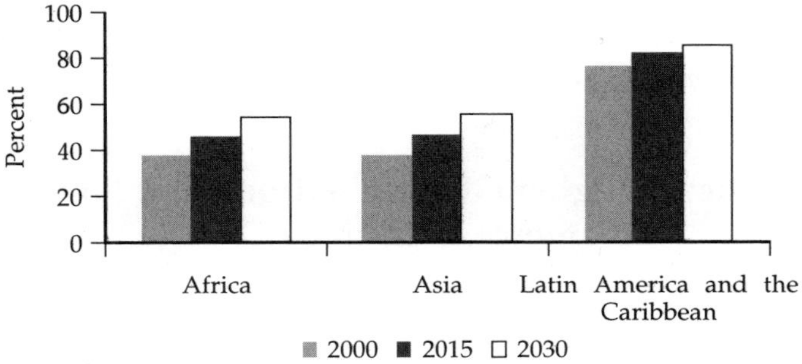

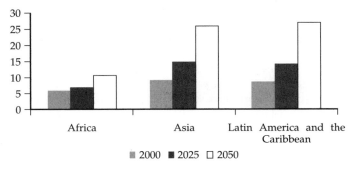

Source: UN 2002.

Soviet Union and Latin America. Some countries in these regions are now experiencing an absolute decline in rural labor as wage differentials draw labor out of agriculture and push farm labor costs up.

The chronic health problems experienced by rural people living in poverty also affect the size and productivity of the agricultural labor force. These health problems are many, but HIV/AIDS in particular threatens the progress made in agricultural development over the past 40 years, especially in Africa. By 2020, Sub-Saharan Africa could lose up to 25 percent of its agricultural labor force, with disastrous consequences for food production and rural livelihoods. HIV/AIDS does not simply deprive families of important household providers; it draws time and resources from care-

Figure 2.6 Percent of Total Population Over 60

Source: UN 2002.

givers, undermines the transfer of knowledge and farming skills across generations, and threatens the social fabric of communities. Women already head about one-third of rural households in Africa, and in some areas only children and the elderly can tend the fields. It is important to recognize that better rural health depends on improved food production and higher incomes.

The Changing Global Environment: From Commerce to Climate Change

Agricultural trade policies as well as a changing climate presents the agriculture sector with new challenges.

The International Trade Environment: A Tax on Development

Rapid growth in the world economy has been driven in part by an even faster rise in international trade, catalyzed by technological breakthroughs and trade liberalization. Because agriculture has a larger tradable component than most sectors, it is profoundly affected by the trade environment and trade policy. Whereas overall trade barriers in industrial countries have declined significantly over the last decade, the remaining barriers are concentrated on agricultural products and labor-intensive manufactures in which developing countries have a comparative advantage. High levels of farm support, at the level of US$238 billion per year (a billion is 1,000 million) in countries belonging to the Organisation for Economic Co-operation and Development (OECD), depress world prices for several key commodities (especially sugar, cotton, milk, and beef) and deeply undermine agricultural growth in developing countries (box 2.5).

Quotas and tariffs remain important instruments for protection, and sanitary and phytosanitary restrictions increasingly perform the same function (see chapter 3). Tariff rate quotas still protect 28 percent of OECD's agricultural production (a figure that is probably underestimated; see de Gorter and Hranaiova 2004). Although the average tariff on agricultural products is reported to be 10 to 20 percent, extremely high tariffs (up to 500 percent) on specific agricultural imports are reducing market opportunities for developing country farmers. Moreover, escalating tariff structures, which place higher tariffs on more processed products, are widespread. These tariffs protect processing industries in industrialized countries and amount to a tax on development, because they limit developing countries to producing low value-added primary products. For example, to enter the European Union (EU) and Japanese markets, fully

Box 2.5 The Winners: High Levels of Producer Support in OECD Countries

Average producer support equivalents in 2001–3 amounted to US$44 billion (United States), US$102 billion (EU), and US$44 billion (Japan) (total support being considerably higher). These producer subsidy equivalents vary greatly among commodities: rice (80 percent of production value), milk and sugar (around 50 percent), wheat and mutton (40 percent), beef (33 percent), maize and oilseeds (25 percent), and pork and poultry (20 percent). On average, prices received by OECD farmers were 31 percent above world prices, and almost one-third of total farm income originated from government programs. Of this support, 68 percent is administered via price support and output payments—the most distorting mechanisms and most harmful for developing country farmers.

Source: OECD 2004.

processed manufactured food products face tariffs twice as large as products in their first stage of processing.

These policies impose net costs to taxpayers, consumers, and the environment, and they can have large negative implications for producers in developing countries (box 2.6). Current World Trade Organization (WTO) negotiations seek significant reductions in all types of barriers to agricultural trade, including barriers to market access, export subsidies, and trade-distorting domestic support. Probably the biggest challenge is to level the playing

Box 2.6 The Losers: Cotton Subsidies and the Cost to African Farmers

In Sub-Saharan Africa, where cotton is produced by millions of rural poor, the distortions created by U.S. domestic subsidies of US$3.4 billion have led to overproduction and have brought international prices to a 30-year low. Many farmers in West and Central Africa, who can produce cotton for about 75 percent less than U.S. farmers, have been displaced by the U.S. subsidies. It is estimated that the subsidies have cost poor farmers in the region US$301 million and that 10 to 11 million households have been negatively affected. In Benin alone, prices would rise by 25 percent and 250,000 people would be lifted out of poverty if U.S. subsidies were eliminated.

Source: IFAD 2004.

field in agricultural trade by reducing trade-distorting agricultural subsidies in developed countries and strengthening developing countries' positions in future trade negotiations. In practice, the high costs of negotiation and the lack of technical capacity in many developing countries will limit their collective ability to negotiate development-friendly rules for trade or to resolve disputes through WTO and other international bodies.[1]

New International Agreements Change the Rules for the Rural Poor

The proliferation of new international agreements and treaties has direct implications for agriculture and presents a variety of challenges and opportunities for primary producers in developing countries (box 2.7). Agreements are emerging to regulate resources shared by multiple countries, to better protect property rights, to allow collective action at the regional level, to provide regional and global public goods and services, and to strengthen linkages to global markets.

Governments, the private sector, and civil society need to understand the implications of such agreements, need to have the institutional capacity to implement their relevant provisions, and need to maintain the ability to formulate and present views in future negotiations. The challenge is to build capacity so that public officials can evaluate potential negotiating positions and their likely implications for various groups, with particular emphasis on the poor and vulnerable. Another major challenge, not only for public officials but also for the private sector (including farmers), will be to strengthen national capacity to implement these agreements.

Climate Change Will Redefine Agriculture

According to FAO (2003b), some of the poorest developing countries could be most adversely affected by climate change, whereas some industrialized countries may actually benefit. Crop yields could decline by one-fifth in many developing countries. The availability of water—particularly in the subtropics—is expected to diminish, and interannual seasonal variation will increase and have a large effect on the poor. The frequency and intensity of droughts, flooding, and other extreme weather events are expected to grow. Reduced rainfall, higher temperatures, and changing pest populations will reduce food production in much of the tropics. The crops, livestock, homes, food stores, and livelihoods of the poor will be at greater risk from floods and droughts, and the poor have few or no savings to carry them through bad periods.

Although global climate change has important implications for future production patterns, current agricultural practices themselves contribute to climate

---

Box 2.7 International Agreements Are a Force for Change in Agriculture

Through a variety of agreements, the international community has addressed many issues facing the agricultural sector. Key agreements, conventions, treaties, or protocols that affect agriculture include:

- *International Plant Protection Convention (1951)*
- *International Code of Conduct on the Distribution and Use of Pesticides (1985)*
- *International Code of Conduct for Plant Germplasm Collecting and Transfer (1993)*
- *World Trade Organization (WTO) Agreement on Agriculture (1995) and related Sanitary and Phyto-Sanitary Agreement (1995)*
- *WTO Trade Related Intellectual Property (TRIPS) Agreement (1995)*
- *Code of Conduct for Responsible Fisheries (1995)*
- *United Nations Convention to Combat Desertification (1996)*
- *World Food Summit: Rome Declaration and Plan of Action (1996)*
- *Cartagena Protocol on Biosafety (2000)*
- *Stockholm Convention on Persistent Organic Pollutants (POPs) (2001)*
- *International Treaty on Plant Genetic Resources for Food and Agriculture (2001)*
- *Principles for the Risk Analysis of Foods Derived from Modern Biotechnology (2003)*

Negotiations continue on a number of issues, including market standards, subsidies, and market access for agricultural trade (WTO).

Sources: WEHAB Working Group 2002; Authors.

---

change. Agriculture accounts for about 30 percent of the global greenhouse gas emissions resulting from human activity, with irrigated farming systems and ruminant livestock production being the most important contributors. It will be a major challenge to adjust production systems to the changing biophysical environment while mitigating the adverse environmental effects of agricultural practices and fostering practices with beneficial effects.

Who's Who in Agriculture: Changing Players, Changing Partners

The roles of the large number of stakeholders with an interest in the agricultural sector are also changing.

The Public and Private Sector: Shifting the Balance of Activities

The trends toward market liberalization, the rise of supply chains, and the imposition of more rigid grades and standards have changed the role of government in agriculture. Formerly governments functioned as active participants in production, processing, and trade, but increasingly they act as facilitators that develop and enforce the rules by which private sector participants interact within market arenas. Even as current development strategies provide for increased private sector involvement, the quality and efficiency of public policies, institutions, and investments are increasingly critical for the emergence of a modernized and competitive agriculture.

The major tasks for the public sector include

- implementing unfinished reforms, such as restructuring public bureaucracies and devolving programs to lower levels of government;
- formulating, facilitating, and implementing coherent national agricultural development strategies and programs;
- developing mechanisms for producers and the private sector to participate in formulating and implementing policies and programs;
- financing core public goods and services, such as agricultural R&D, food safety, infrastructure, and sustainable natural resource management; and
- carrying out regulatory, information, policy, and negotiation functions to promote efficient markets and respond to international agreements and standards.

In many cases, the private sector has successfully replaced inefficient public or parastatal agencies as a supplier of essentially private services, including the distribution of agricultural inputs and the processing and marketing of farm products. The transition to private sector leadership has been successful when effective rules govern market and private sector behavior. Many government functions are being contracted out to specialized private firms and NGOs under competitive bidding. Governments are also partnering with NGOs, private organizations of producers and water users, and trade associations to formulate policy, regulate food safety, and provide and manage irrigation and other infrastructure.

In other cases, however, the public sector's withdrawal from these essentially private activities has left a vacuum. Where private initiative has not stepped in because of some combination of failed markets and policies, agricultural performance and the prospects of the poor have been seriously undermined. Especially in many African countries, where markets function poorly because of poor infrastructure, high risks, and high transactions costs, the emergence of private markets in agricultural inputs and outputs has been blocked (Dorward et al. 2004). An important challenge is to address these failures, ensuring appropriate transitional arrangements that may require some involvement of the public sector, but aiming for a medium- to long-term strategy that creates an enabling environment for private investment.

Civil Society: Shifting the Balance of Power

Initiatives in agriculture and rural development must recognize the growing importance of civil society[2] in ensuring that the poor participate in political processes, market opportunities, and policy debates on agricultural growth. The specific objectives of civil society organizations vary, but they generally relate to serving and protecting their own interests or those of the constituencies that they represent. Their programs range from highly localized, practical activities to broad participation in national policy making. They are particularly important for voicing the concerns of people who have limited political influence, who are often poor and involved in agriculture.

Civil society organizations can help address the imbalance of power between poorly organized farmers and powerful public and private operators, which often diminishes poor people's ability to adjust to new economic conditions. Rural producer organizations (RPOs) address this problem by building social capital among members and increasing their voice in public sector decision making and market activities. As a result of decentralization, RPOs are increasingly able to influence public service delivery and the nature of development initiatives.

Like RPOs, NGOs often provide services to poor producers, but unlike RPOs, NGOs directly serve nonmembers and often have an international scope of operations. Many NGOs have unique competencies in developing regions, and donors increasingly utilize their resources and capabilities. NGOs are usually connected to local organizations and may strongly influence national policy as well.[3]

Rapid Change and the Need for New Approaches

In summary, what changes are in store for agriculture in the years to come, and what are some of the implications for farmers, governments, and others concerned with development? A number of global forces will command the attention of the development community because of their strong effect on economic growth, poverty, and the supply of agricultural commodities. These forces include climate change, demographic trends, health issues (especially HIV/AIDS), the degradation of natural resources, and rapidly changing technologies and markets.

Box 2.8 Is Agriculture's Role in Pro-Poor Growth Now Different?

Agriculture's pro-poor role in the structural transformation process was demonstrated in the wake of the green revolution. The successful transformation of many economies in the decades that followed, especially in Asia, saw agriculture's share in national economies decline. The steady fall of commodity prices in world markets to an all-time low in recent years, the lack of obvious technological breakthroughs in agriculture, the growing importance of trade in a globalizing economy, and the growing role of rural nonfarm income have all raised questions about agriculture's ability to deliver pro-poor growth.

Is this "agro-pessimism" justified? A multidonor group led by the World Bank recently completed a comprehensive study of pro-poor growth based on 14 country case studies. The evidence from the case studies, in the context of the wider development literature, has led to five broad propositions about how and when agriculture and rural development contribute to pro-poor growth:

1. *Agriculture has played an important and often a lead role in the early stages of pro-poor growth.* Beyond its direct contribution to growth, a number of features specific to agriculture enhance its contribution to pro-poor growth, including the concentration of the poor in the sector, its very large growth links to other sectors, and the positive consequences of food security and lower food prices.
2. The contribution of agriculture to growth naturally declines as agricultural economies are transformed into urban-based, nonagricultural economies, but even in countries that have attained solid, middle-income status, *agriculture continues to "pull beyond its weight,"* as measured by its contribution to GDP, because of its unique "externalities."
3. *The rural nonfarm economy increasingly becomes a source of growth and contributes to rural incomes,* initially because of its links to agricultural growth and later because of increasing ties with urban-industrial development, especially in densely populated areas where infrastructure is good.
4. *Rural development remains critical to reducing poverty and inequality,* even as agriculture's role in growth declines during structural transformation. Differences in natural resource endowments, access to markets, and access to assets often promote uneven growth and growing inequality within the sector that must be addressed explicitly through poverty-oriented rural development strategies.

(box continued next page)

(box continued)

5. *More than ever, local contexts matter.* Agriculture's contribution to pro-poor growth varies enormously, not only at different stages of development in a given country, but also across and within countries. *Local contexts must condition the design of public policy for enhancing the contribution of agriculture and rural development to pro-poor growth.*

Source: Byerlee et al. 2005.

Agriculture contributed greatly to reducing poverty and transforming economies after the green revolution, but farmers and economies have changed considerably since then. Given the agricultural challenges described in this chapter, and given that agriculture is changing rapidly as economies develop (see the discussion on structural transformation in chapter 1), some have come to question whether agriculture remains a reliable pathway to pro-poor growth.

Although agriculture does continue to support pro-poor growth as economies develop, much can be learned from studying how and when this occurs (box 2.8). If farm households are to seize emerging opportunities in agriculture or pursue better opportunities outside agriculture, business as usual is not an option. The public sector is no longer the main driver of development.

Table 2.1 Changing Emphasis in Agricultural Growth Strategies in the World Bank's Rural Strategy

Less emphasis	*More emphasis*
Resource- and input-led growth	Knowledge-led growth and sustainable production systems
Agricultural production	Agricultural supply chains and markets
Food staples	Promotion of higher value products, but continued priority for staple crops in low-income countries
Traditional exports	Nontraditional exports
Broad-based approaches	Differentiated strategies to reduce poverty based on the level of development and type of agricultural enterprise

Source: Adapted from World Bank 2003b.

It must work in close partnership with the private sector, NGOs, civil society, and international donor and finance organizations to develop novel approaches that smooth the transition from traditional production practices to systems that are more aligned with current markets and growing scarcities of natural resources. If the public sector cannot effectively work through these partnerships, agriculture will not fulfill its potential to serve the larger economy or the poor.

Some specific changes in agricultural growth strategy are highlighted in the World Bank's Rural Strategy, *Reaching the Rural Poor* (table 2.1). The chapters that follow will provide details of new approaches and entry points for the international development community, particularly the World Bank, to support agricultural development where it will have the greatest positive impact on the lives of the poor. Chapter 3 focuses on a range of prospective policies and institutions, chapter 4 focuses on investments, and chapter 5 looks more closely at how priorities for policies, institutions, and investments change depending on the agricultural system for which they are intended.

3

Policies and Institutions to Accelerate Agricultural Growth for the Poor

In this chapter

What policies and institutions are needed to generate economic growth that is distributed in socially desirable ways?

- A significant agenda for trade and market reforms remains to be addressed at the global and national level. Internationally, much can be done to advocate changes that level the playing field for all countries and to improve the negotiating positions of developing countries in international agreements. Even in the current global trade environment, developing countries generally will gain from liberalizing their own trade policies. However, complementary policies will be needed to facilitate adjustment and to provide safety nets for those who lose out in the liberalization process.
- Market and trade liberalization alone will not promote growth that reduces poverty. Institutional development is a priority for growth and poverty reduction, but it cannot occur without a long-term, sustained commitment. Much has been learned over the last several decades about building institutions in the agricultural sector. Decentralization, empowerment of users, and inclusiveness are essential features of institutions that promote growth and reduce poverty, especially strong producer, community, and other types of local organizations.
- Public policy should support institutional arrangements that lower the costs of transactions to provide private goods (e.g., secure and tradable rights for land and water, contract enforcement). The public sector in particular will need to expand its range of partnerships and alter the way it participates in institutional development. A growing array of public-private partnerships requires the state to shift from providing services directly to coordinating, facilitating, building capacity, and developing regulations. The private sector should lead developments

(box continued next page)

(box continued)

in areas such as rural finance and insurance, but the public sector has a key role in providing an enabling environment and very selective, up-front services.

- Nationally owned agricultural and rural strategies are important for integrating sector reforms and priorities, and for building stakeholders' support for the reform process.

Globally and nationally, the three keys to broad-based agricultural development are policies that promote private investment and market development, appropriate institutions,[1] and public goods that stimulate private investment while empowering poor and marginalized people to participate in economic growth. This chapter presents general principles for guiding initiatives to improve policies and institutions in agriculture under the broad range of circumstances encountered in developing countries. It presents brief case studies of many individual policy and institutional initiatives and distills the lessons that they present. The distinct and complementary roles of the public and private sectors and civil society in supporting the development of policies and institutions are discussed as well.

Another prerequisite for long-term, strong, and equitable growth is investment in the core public goods that society requires but that the market fails to supply, especially infrastructure, R&D, and human resources. These are discussed in greater detail in chapter 4. Together, policies, institutions, and investments in public goods create an environment in which markets guide the allocation of resources to generate economic growth that is distributed in socially desirable ways. Inadequacies in any one of these three areas can stall growth or exclude poor people from any growth that does occur. For example, even if policy establishes a framework that encourages private investment, investment can still be frustrated by high transactions costs and the lack of complementary investments. Policies and institutions will fail if mechanisms are not in place to ensure broad participation. This chapter and the next provide many other examples of the interdependence of policies, institutions, and investments and the implications for designing effective agricultural strategies.

Promoting the Global Agenda

Global policies and institutions governing trade, knowledge sharing, and environmental protection are particularly relevant to the agricultural sector. These policies and institutions produce international public goods that transcend national boundaries. Examples of these public goods are international trade regulations, knowledge and technologies needed to improve agricultural productivity, and environmental agreements.

Global Trade Policies to Foster Development

An enduring challenge for the development community is to support the creation of a trading system that favors development. By setting bounds on the policies of wealthier as well as poorer countries, international trade rules have the potential to promote economic growth in developing countries, but the current reality is that rules often fail to support the interests of the poorest countries. International agricultural trade rules are especially contentious because most high- and middle-income countries enact policies to protect the dwindling but politically powerful population of their own farmers (see chapter 2). Developed countries' subsidies, tariffs, and restricted markets cause prices to fall and generate enormous pressure within developing countries to retaliate with protective measures of their own.

The cost of maintaining this uneven playing field is considerable, and much of it is borne by developing countries. Because developing country exports face higher trade barriers, and their agricultural sectors are relatively large, they stand to gain significantly from multilateral trade liberalization. Global agricultural trade reform would bring about an aggregate welfare gain of some US$142 billion per year in developing countries (figure 3.1) (World Bank 2002). *Most of these gains, about US$114 billion, would come from trade policy reforms within developing countries themselves.*

Aside from the potential conflicts arising from inequalities in the current trading system, negotiations on agricultural trade are complicated by the special cultural, health, and security attributes of food, and by the multiple roles of farming (e.g., farming provides not just food but environmental services as well). As noted in the previous chapter, the specific details of regulations such as sanitary and phytosanitary (SPS) restrictions are gaining importance among exporters of higher-value products because they have such a strong influence on access to markets (box 3.1). Despite their growing importance, these regulations are far from uniform. The lack of global technical standards, along with the difficulty of proving "equivalence"[2] of processes, create confusion and can discourage trade. For instance, some countries apply international (Codex Alimentarius)

Figure 3.1 Income Gains from Accelerated Trade Liberalization

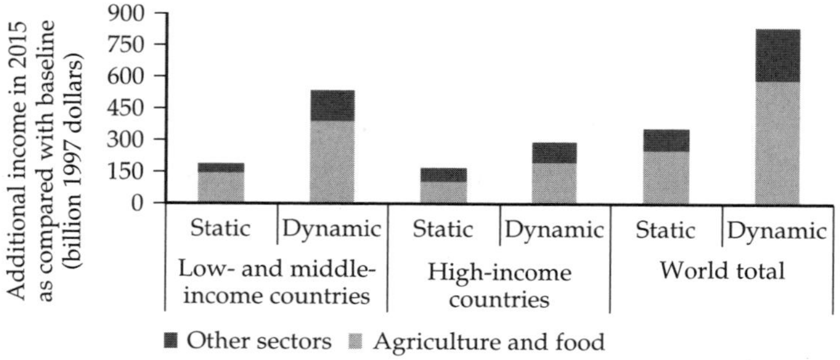

Source: World Bank 2002.
Note: Static gains refer to results holding productivity constant. Dynamic gains allow productivity to respond to sector-specific export-to-output ratios.

standards for maximum residue levels (MRLs) of pesticides, whereas others apply their own, often stricter, MRLs. Sometimes SPS requirements for agricultural products are far more stringent than justified by the risks involved and actually become barriers to trade. A number of import controls that involve phytosanitary issues for horticultural products have been reported to the WTO (FAO 2004b). In some cases, standards set by private buyers are even more important constraints than these public standards.

Box 3.1 Nile Perch and the Upstream Battle to Meet Safety Standards

European safety standards have periodically restricted imports of Nile perch from Kenya and elsewhere in East Africa. From November 1996 to April 1997, imports to Spain and Italy ceased after salmonella was detected in a number of consignments. A requirement for salmonella testing for Nile perch from the region was introduced. An outbreak of cholera in the region in the second half of 1997 led to further suspension of Nile perch imports from December 1997 to June 1998, until fish could be tested for the cholera virus. A suspected case of fish poisoning by pesticide in Uganda led the EU to ban imports of fresh and frozen Nile perch again in March 1999. Restrictions were lifted only in December 2000, after EU inspections of improved Kenyan facilities.

Source: Henson and Mitullah 2003.

Aside from SPS standards, exporters must deal with other international technical regulations, including certification requirements, labeling requirements, and environmental standards. Many developing countries simply lack the resources to participate in developing technical standards or to prove the "equivalence" of their products and production processes. For some products, it is inadvisable for developing countries to seek similar standards for export and domestic markets, as local food preparation preferences make international standards irrelevant.

Global trade issues differ greatly in importance among developing countries and can sometimes limit incentives to join in negotiations. Among cotton- and sugar-exporting countries, rich countries' subsidies and high tariffs are contentious issues that have yet to be fully resolved through the WTO. Many of the poorest countries, on the other hand, are concerned with finding the balance between relying on food aid or commercial food imports, or managing the risks of unstable prices of a critical food staple. Although under certain circumstances WTO rules permit countries to help producers adjust to sharp movements in world prices, the current formulation of many such rules within WTO makes them inappropriate for developing countries (Foster and Valdés 2004). For countries that import food, dealing with the outcomes of such negotiations will be especially important, because global trade liberalization will raise world market prices of cereals.

Global Policies to Create and Share Knowledge

New knowledge developed through agricultural R&D, such as an improved method for breeding more nutritious crops or conserving soil moisture, has public good elements that spill across national boundaries. *A central feature of the agricultural development agenda should be internationally funded research to develop global public goods that reduce poverty and hunger.* It is often much more efficient to organize this kind of strategic research at the international or regional level than at the country level in order to capture significant economies of size.

The realization that agricultural research for small-scale farmers was an international public good with high potential for reducing hunger and poverty was a primary motive for establishing the Consultative Group on International Agricultural Research (CGIAR) and its constituent research centers. The record of the CGIAR centers in developing and disseminating new knowledge for agriculture has more than justified their costs (box 3.2). Although the challenge of making agriculture more diversified, intensive, and environmentally friendly will require continued strong support to the CGIAR centers, a change in their agenda is required. They must conduct more long-term strategic research, especially

---

**Box 3.2 Major Contributions by CGIAR
to International Agricultural Research**

The Consultative Group on International Agricultural Research (CGIAR)
has made major contributions to developing and disseminating new
knowledge for agriculture. The results from more than 35 years of investments in CGIAR include

- developing more than 300 varieties of wheat and rice and over
  200 varieties of maize that have supported the doubling of global
  food production and improved health and nutrition for millions of
  people;
- preserving the world's largest collection of plant genetic resources;
- training more than 75,000 scientists and technical experts from developing countries; and
- developing technologies that have saved more than 200 million
  hectares of land from cultivation.

Conservative estimates of the return on past investments in CGIAR
centers suggest that for every dollar spent in the CGIAR system, nine dol-
lars of additional food has been produced in the developing world.

Sources: Raitzer 2003; www.cgiar.org.

---

in biotechnology, that will enable agriculture to grow in the future. Currently their capacity to conduct strategic research has been limited by
changes in donor funding mechanisms and reduced capacity for national
agricultural research in some regions (World Bank 2003g).

The urgency for CGIAR to invest more substantially in biotechnology is
increasing. The private sector now accounts for 70 percent of the research
spending on genomics and 80 percent of the patents emanating from this
research. Private companies supplying agricultural inputs, such as seed or
veterinary medicines, spend at least 20 times more on agricultural
research globally than the CGIAR (Pardey and Beintema 2001). Because
the private sector naturally tends to focus on commercial agriculture and
restrict access to research results, the knowledge and technology divide
between the developed and developing world, and between private and
public research organizations, is becoming far more extreme. The World
Bank has been a prime advocate for bridging that divide by opening
CGIAR to broader partnerships with the private sector. CGIAR's four
new Challenge Programs seek to combine traditional public funding with
support from private organizations. Two of the Challenge Programs will

enhance CGIAR's competence in genomics and biotechnology. One of the programs has attracted significant private funding.[3]

Global Environmental Policies Could Benefit Marginal Agricultural Areas

A number of global agreements (see box 2.8) address transnational environmental problems. These agreements directly affect the use and international valuation of environmental resources and services that are concentrated in the agricultural sector, such as biodiversity and carbon sequestration.

Some global agreements offer much potential to empower poor farmers to "market" global environmental services (box 3.3). This is especially important in marginal areas where people have virtually no prospect of earning an income outside of agriculture. For example, markets for carbon emissions trading are being developed to counter global warming. They may create opportunities to sell carbon sequestration services in developing countries, which are responsible for only a small share of global carbon emissions but have enormous potential for sequestering carbon in agricultural and ecological systems. The details of carbon trading markets are still being negotiated,

---

Box 3.3 Selling Environmental Services in Latin America

Deforestation in Colombia, Costa Rica, and Nicaragua has been high. The Global Environment Facility funds a project that provides incentive payments to farmers who adopt silvopastoral techniques on degraded pasturelands. These techniques include replanting degraded lands with trees, legumes, and fast-growing shrubs that are environmentally sound and financially productive. The project is implemented by the World Bank, through NGOs in Costa Rica (Center for Tropical Agriculture), Colombia (Center for Sustainable Agriculture), and Nicaragua (Nitlapan of the University of Central America).

The volume of environmental services is estimated using landscape changes as a proxy for the amount of carbon and enhanced biodiversity accumulated. Changes in land use are measured rapidly and objectively using satellite and Global Positioning System technology. The project pays farmers only *after* they have changed their land-use practices. Sustaining payments in the long term might involve earmarked general tax funds or cost recovery from those benefiting directly from the environmental services, such as municipalities that benefit from improved water quality.

Source: World Bank 2004b.

---

and whether poor farmers benefit will depend to a great extent on how effectively developing countries manage these negotiations.

Entry Points for Global Public Policy

A major global agenda in trade, knowledge, and the environment still needs to be addressed to reduce poverty and foster economic growth. Current international support for this reform agenda is extremely modest compared with the contributions that global efforts actually can make. Although multilateral and even bilateral development agencies generally have little direct leverage in discussions on these issues, the development community, including the World Bank, can redouble efforts to reduce trade barriers in industrialized and developing countries. Success in leveling the playing field for developing country farmers in international trade is fundamental to realizing agriculture's potential to reduce poverty.

The development community can also provide support and build capacity so that developing countries improve their negotiating position in trade agreements. The World Bank and its partners must continue their wide-ranging analyses of how subsidies and protection affect specific commodities, such as cotton and sugar, that are important for small-scale farmers in the developing world. A global accord that curtails trade-distorting subsidies on these commodities will directly improve the incomes of the world's poorest farmers.

Developing countries have a range of strategic options at the international level for improving market access, maintaining competitiveness and productivity, and managing risks. These options include voicing their concerns through complaints in international forums such as the WTO, deepening participation in efforts to regulate trade and set standards, pursuing changes that ensure compliance with evolving standards, exiting sectors with increasingly stringent standards, or some combination of these alternatives. Generally the most successful strategy has been for public and private entities to act cooperatively in a proactive rather than a reactive way to achieve these goals (World Bank 2005c).

Public and private sector collaboration is also vital for international agricultural research, especially in supporting more strategic, longer term initiatives. The World Bank's advocacy of reform in international agricultural research can catalyze the development of new synergies with agribusiness and other private sector partners. The international community's support for international agricultural research through CGIAR needs to be sustained, ensuring that CGIAR focuses on international public goods of most benefit to the poor and increases its partnerships with the private sector.

Finally, developing countries may benefit from international environmental accords by participating in efforts to develop markets for global environmental services. Service provision could provide alternative sources of income to poor farmers, especially in marginal agricultural areas.

An Agenda for Policies and Institutions at the National Level

Changes in global policies and institutions can open new avenues for development and for reducing poverty, but the effects of these avenues will be attenuated without highly focused policies and effective institutions at the national and local levels. This section examines the role of macroeconomic and agricultural policies in promoting private investment, ensuring responsible environmental stewardship, and protecting the interests of poor and disenfranchised people who will be severely challenged by agricultural and socioeconomic change. It also discusses the institutions that are needed to foster market-oriented agriculture in ways that do not exclude the poor. For example, producers will need institutions that empower them and allow for decentralized decision making and collective action. Producers also need institutional arrangements to access modern technology and information and to provide them with clear market signals and better access to markets. Financial and risk management institutions will enable them to adopt improved technologies and participate in supply chains. The sections that follow present a detailed review of options that decision makers can pursue to improve the policy and institutional environment for agriculture.

Macroeconomic and Trade Policies to Strengthen Agriculture

In the past, farm profitability and the performance of the agricultural sector were greatly weakened by overvalued exchange rates, high inflation, and food prices that were set to favor urban consumers. Although most of these distortions have been removed, in some countries inappropriate macroeconomic policy remains a major barrier to agricultural performance and economic growth (box 3.4).

The effects of inappropriate policies are of particular concern in the agricultural sector, where reform—especially in agricultural trade policies—has been slower than in other sectors. It is in a country's interest to take the initiative in trade liberalization. Trade-oriented countries consistently grow faster than those that protect their economies from imports. High levels of protection make it much more difficult for a country to make the transition to higher-value agricultural activities or to move labor into nonagricultural sectors where

---

Box 3.4 República Bolivariana de Venezuela: The Negative Impacts of Inappropriate Macroeconomic Policy

Over time, policies in República Bolivariana de Venezuela have become more interventionist, protectionist, and discretionary. Exchange rate controls, including the restriction of currency transactions and the imposition of an official exchange rate, have limited agricultural competitiveness and food security. Major impediments to the development of the agricultural sector include price ceilings for many goods; import licensing and nontariff barriers, as well as restrictions on exports to ensure enough domestic supply; government importation and distribution of food; and agricultural price controls. This constellation of policies has had a number of undesirable results. Black markets have appeared. Agricultural and food products are smuggled into the country. The cost of doing business has increased. Progress in raising per capita food production, increasing exports, improving the agro-food commercial balance, improving household food security, and reducing rural poverty has been below expectations.

Source: World Bank internal documents.

---

workers may be more productive. To the extent that they distort producers' incentives, national trade policies increasingly threaten future agricultural growth and environmental welfare in many developing countries. *There is a growing consensus that creating high import barriers (tariff or nontariff) in the name of food security or to support an import-substitution agricultural development strategy is bad policy for long-term growth. In addition, in agriculture:*

- The cost to poor consumers from protectionism is higher for food than for many other products, since the poor spend a much larger share of their limited income on food;
- The rural poor benefit from the protection of food crops less than it would appear, because the poorest are often small-scale farmers who are net food purchasers or landless laborers who are hurt by higher food prices.[4]
- Food security is less a supply-side problem, caused by insufficient food crop production, than a demand-side problem caused by insufficient purchasing power.

Free trade generally benefits the poor over the long term, although not all poor people come out ahead. Production systems that provided reliable livelihoods for generations may suddenly become unprofitable,

although new opportunities often emerge for producers who can reallo-
cate their resources to take advantage of them. When poor people lack the
assets or knowledge to take advantage of new opportunities, or when
policies or institutions constrain them from doing so, they suffer in the
short term. It is imperative to identify constraints on the poor and to promote efficient, equitable adjustment to changing markets. *For developing
countries, the strategy should be to sequence trade liberalization in a way that:*

- minimizes short-term adverse effects on the economy;
- includes support for vulnerable groups, to ensure that they benefit
  from the growth process and sustain political support for it; and
- supports pro-active rather than reactive policy in trade negotiations.

*Some general principles are useful to guide countries in designing and pacing
trade reform:*

- *First,* the size and "tradability" of the sector matters. A rapid reduction
  in protection for a sector that is a large and tradable part of the economy can generate significant unemployment and hardship.
- *Second,* the pattern of protection matters. Where agricultural protection is uneven and biased toward a few sensitive commodities, the case
  for reducing protection is stronger than it is when protection is spread
  over many products. If protection is concentrated, farmers and labor
  can shift more easily to the large number of commodities for which
  there is little protection.
- *Third,* although the downward price effects of subsidies, tariffs, and
  restrictions on market access by developed countries creates pressure
  on developing countries to maintain a protectionist stance, this
  response is economically justified only in very specific circumstances.
  For example, modest, short-term protection, with a clear exit policy
  and time limit, may be justified when there is clear potential for developing competitive agricultural industries and where a high likelihood
  of reduced protection in world markets in the short- to medium-term
  would cause world prices to rise.
- *Fourth,* attention needs to focus on the question of what kinds of complementary policies are necessary and feasible to provide safety nets
  and facilitate adjustment, how quickly they can be implemented, and
  when and how they should come to an end.

One role for complementary policies is to manage the price risks that
arise in a more liberalized trading environment. Market-based alternatives for managing price risk, such as commercial forward and futures
markets for certain commodities, offer some potential (see the discussion

later in this chapter). For sensitive commodities, including food staples, price bands and price floors might be used. Price floors help to prevent extreme hardship in years when world prices are extremely low. Similarly, price bands help to stabilize prices between a floor and a ceiling. It is important to caution, however, that although these schemes are based on solid theoretical underpinnings, they have produced mixed results in practice. Current WTO rules on safeguards also restrict their applicability (Foster and Valdés 2004).

Another complementary strategy to ease the adjustment to lower levels of protection is to support the incomes of the poor directly, in a way that is not linked to production. Such "decoupled" support programs provide assistance to farmers without raising food prices or encouraging recipients to remain in unproductive activities. They offer fixed and guaranteed payments to recipients, usually per hectare up to a maximum area. In countries where decoupled support programs are feasible, tariffs can be reduced and other subsidies can be phased out relatively quickly. Experience in Mexico (box 3.5) and Turkey shows that this approach can be practical for some countries. Many countries may not be able to afford direct payments, however, or they may lack the institutions (in particular, a land registration system) needed to implement them. In these cases, protection may need to be reduced more gradually.

In middle-income countries that face reduced employment in agriculture but still experience extensive rural poverty, one alternative is to provide direct support that enables producers to leave agriculture (although not necessarily rural areas). Recurrent transfers (ideally in return for some environmental or social service) might be appropriate in some cases. More typically, programs to help producers leave inefficient agricultural subsectors and reduce poverty involve one-time payments and training services to prepare people for employment in other sectors, rural and urban. Public works programs, government distribution of resources in-kind, cash payments, and social funds can all be used to help those who are most likely to be adversely affected. Improved transportation and communication systems are a less direct means of helping people to leave agriculture, whether to the rural nonfarm economy or to urban centers. Whatever compensatory policies are adopted, in-depth analytical work based on detailed household surveys is usually needed to target assistance to the groups that are vulnerable to the effects of trade liberalization.

Reforming Input Subsidies and Price Supports

Agricultural programs historically provided inputs and services directly through state agencies, most of which performed poorly and many of

---

**Box 3.5 Mexico: Cash Transfer Programs Benefit
Smallholders without Distorting Production Incentives**

Mexico introduced the Program for Direct Assistance to Agriculture (PRO-CAMPO) to compensate producers for the reduction in prices of agricultural commodities that would occur when the North American Free Trade Agreement (NAFTA) came into effect. PROCAMPO, introduced in 1994, had objectives that were political (to increase the political acceptability of free trade), economic (to provide farmers with the liquidity to adjust production to a new set of relative prices), and social (to soften the impact of removing producer price supports). Under PROCAMPO, individuals receive twice-yearly payments based on area cropped in one of three seasons prior to 1993. Because payments are not related to current farming activities, they do not distort production incentives. The payouts can be used to purchase inputs, invest in productive assets, or leave farming entirely. Moreover, because the payments do not relate to volumes sold, small-scale farmers benefit more than other producer groups (payments are given for a minimum of 1 hectare regardless of actual farm size, and for a maximum of 100 hectares). In 1997, the average annual value of payments was around 8 percent of household income, and for the poorest decile, around 40 percent. Although positive, these benefits would have been higher if payments had been made on time and if they had been accompanied by complementary initiatives to use transfers more productively (for example, through improvements in credit institutions and land tenure systems).

Sources: Sadoulet, de Janvry, and Davis 2001; Baffes and de Gorter 2005.

---

which have been closed as countries seek to implement market reforms. Some countries, however, rushed to implement reforms despite a poor business environment that prevented the private sector from filling the void left by the parastatals. This problem has been particularly acute in the least-developed countries. To avoid such negative outcomes, policies to liberalize or privatize marketing functions must be carefully phased and must include institutional mechanisms designed to keep markets competitive, provide support services, facilitate private investment and the provision of private goods, and ensure that markets remain free of political interference (box 3.6).

Governments have also traditionally supported farmers through input subsidies. Subsidies may be useful in the transition to a more liberalized trading environment, but when maintained over the longer run, they reduce equity and efficiency (box 3.7). Because subsidized inputs typically cannot be provided in sufficient quantities to meet demand, they

Box 3.6 Benin: Success and Failure
in Reforming the Cotton Sector

Benin's cotton sector accounts for about 7.5 percent of national GDP. Major reforms have been undertaken over the past two decades to move the cotton sector from a state-controlled system to a private one that avoids corruption and fiscal risks while functioning more efficiently and transparently.

From 1980 to 1992: A series of reforms sought to improve the efficiency of the public monopoly, strengthen producer organizations, privatize seed cotton transportation, improve research, and improve export marketing procedures. These reforms increased yields and farmers' incomes.

From 1992 to 1999: Input suppliers and ginneries were privatized, though political interference weakened input supply services. Yields fell, and farmers were unable to adapt, as they received no complementary training.

Since 1999: Additional reforms have included creating agencies to improve coordination within the sector, marketing and recovering credit for inputs, and promoting competition among input suppliers.

Progress improved but only temporarily, because producer organizations dissolved and many ginners proved corrupt. An evaluation using 2003 household survey data suggests that many farmers have stopped producing cotton since 1998, largely due to indebtedness and declining world prices. Although production rebounded in 2003–4, substantial problems persist. These problems include corruption, inefficient extension services, a dysfunctional input system, a lack of capacity to handle production increases, inadequate training and support for farmers during the transition, and political economy issues that must be managed. Future reforms are expected to involve privatizing the remaining ginneries and moving to contract farming, which will expose farmers to international price variability and most likely require price insurance.

Source: World Bank internal documents.

---

must be rationed, which reduces efficiency and tends to favor larger-scale farmers. Small-scale farmers, who are affected the most when the market fails to provide inputs at accessible prices, generally receive the fewest benefits from input subsidies and public intervention in input markets. Finally, market price supports and continued subsidies limit producers' incentives to diversify to higher value products and limit growth in the agricultural sector (box 3.8).

Other strategies have proven to be much more effective than subsidies and price supports in ensuring that small-scale farmers can intensify production and

---

Box 3.7 Two Approaches to Fertilizer Subsidies Yield Contrasting Results

Fertile ground and private fertilizer provision in Bangladesh: During 1988–94, the government of Bangladesh saved about US$119 million by withdrawing fertilizer subsidies. The 800-member Bangladesh Fertilizer Association was created and the fertilizer retail network employed 170,000 people. Fertilizer sales increased at an annual rate of 8 percent, and government fertilizer imports declined from 100 percent to nil. To support the private sector by improving the industry information base, the government instituted monthly monitoring of the fertilizer market.

Infertile ground and public fertilizer provision in Zambia: The overall objective of Zambia's Ministry of Agriculture is to promote a self-sustaining, export-led agricultural sector that ensures increased household incomes and food security. The agricultural programs implemented and reviewed recently during a public expenditure review show that although over 80 percent of the agriculture sector budget was planned to be spent on productive investments and service provision to the sector, the actual expenditures show a different picture. Subsidies (for fertilizer, seed, and the Food Reserve Agency's maize procurement price) accounted for about 70 percent of actual expenditure. Field studies indicated that medium- and larger-scale farmers were the main beneficiaries of these subsidies, while small-scale farmers in remote areas used very little fertilizer. The amount budgeted for subsidies was over 20 times that for agricultural research—a core public good.

Sources: World Bank internal documents.

---

adjust to changing market signals. These strategies include more efficient input distribution through publicly supported infrastructure, packaging standards, low-cost financial services, improved research and extension, and new risk management mechanisms. In many countries, however, public expenditures for these critical public roles continue to be crowded out by input subsidies (box 3.7).

Sudden elimination of input subsidies, however, can cause a radical decline in the use of inputs, especially fertilizer, with potentially devastating effects. Until private input suppliers become established, the public sector must assist poor producers by carefully phasing the removal of subsidies and/or supporting such institutions as voucher systems, which are now being tested in Malawi (box 3.9).

Box 3.8 Policies in the Indian Punjab Discourage Diversification into New Crops

The Indian Punjab became the nation's breadbasket following its leading role in the green revolution in the 1960s and 1970s. A range of federal and state government incentives supported agricultural growth in Punjab, including subsidies on fertilizer, water, and power and minimum support prices for wheat. By the 1990s, these subsidies had become a huge fiscal burden. Because they favored rice and wheat production and discouraged diversification to higher value crop and livestock products, agricultural growth in Punjab slowed to 2.6 percent per year in the 1990s, below the average for all of India. In addition, although 35 percent of farmers have less than 2 hectares (and account for 9 percent of the land area), they receive only 7.5 percent of the fertilizer subsidy, 5.5 percent of the electricity subsidy, and 5 percent of the canal water subsidy.

Source: World Bank (2003f).

Decentralization and Empowerment: Obtaining Larger Impacts from Limited Resources

Unless the poor can influence policies, regulations, and public investments, they will not realize all of the benefits from agricultural growth. *Decentralization of administrative authority is a first step toward empowering the rural poor.* When the responsibility and capacity for delivering services is shifted to the local level, communities can shape public support to match local circumstances and service providers can become more accountable to users. Increased local authority by itself will not ensure that the poor have a voice in local processes or that decision making is fair and transparent, however. For decentralization to bring true empowerment, disadvantaged groups such as ethnic minorities, indigenous populations, women, the landless, the disabled, and refugees must gain greater participation in community-level decision making and prevent local elites from capturing most of the benefits.

Decisions about whether different kinds of public goods should be managed locally or centrally will depend on a clear determination of the nature of the good involved. For example, public goods that are national in scope are best administered by a central government, while those that are more local are usually better controlled at the local level. Thus agricultural grades and standards are most meaningful when they are determined centrally, but soil conservation controls might be better established at the watershed level. Similarly, agricultural extension can best be handled at the local

---

**Box 3.9 Input Voucher Programs Link Poor Farmers
with Private Input Dealers**

Voucher programs to obtain fertilizer and improved seed are a market-
friendly way to target subsidies or crop production credit to poor farmers,
creating links between these farmers and private input dealers. Input
vouchers can function either as a sustainable market development tool or
an emergency market tool. An integral part of voucher programs is the
provision of technical assistance to farmers as well as input dealers.

In *Afghanistan,* IFDC and the U.S. Agency for International Development (USAID) have used vouchers as a post-conflict emergency market
tool for 200,000 small farmers. Fertilizer is provided along with wheat
seed (in association with the International Center for Research in the Dry
Areas, a CGIAR research center) as a crop production credit. Voluntary
post-harvest repayments go to local (village) administrations to invest in
infrastructure.

In *Malawi,* IFDC, with a consortium of NGOs and funding from the
United Kingdom's Department for International Development (DFID) and
the World Bank, has provided 100,000 subsistence farmers with vouchers
to purchase fertilizer. In return, the farmers participate in the NGO-super-
vised construction of feeder roads. This "inputs for assets" approach repre-
sents an alternative to "starter pack" programs formerly funded by donors,
which supplied packets of seed and fertilizer for a small plot free to farmers. Linking recipients with public works programs has been very effective
in targeting the poorest and neediest farmers.

Source: IFDC 2004.

---

level, while control of major pests and diseases can best be managed from
the national level.

*There are many ways to marshall the forces of people with little political or
economic clout to achieve development goals that otherwise would remain elu-
sive.* Rural producer organizations (RPOs) can do much to empower
small-scale agricultural producers to represent their shared interests.
When local organizations such as RPOs are inclusive, they reinforce the
capacity of marginalized people to advocate in favor of their particular
development needs. Large RPOs, usually based on specific commodities,
can influence national policy, while community-based organizations,
including herder groups and water user associations (WUAs), can influence local public investments as well as the regulation and management
of common resources.

For example, the most important step in improving the operation of
irrigation systems occurs when local users become responsible for

operating and managing them. Participatory irrigation management (PIM) has been adopted in more than 50 countries since the 1980s. Recent efforts in Andhra Pradesh in India, Indonesia, and Mexico have supported the operation and financing of public irrigation systems by water users themselves.[5] These evolving forms of PIM have succeeded by creating an adequate policy, legal, and regulatory framework; building a political constituency of support; enhancing the capacity of WUAs and government agencies; and ensuring that WUAs receive the appropriate authority and financial resources to carry out their new responsibilities (World Bank 2005a). Moreover, support for WUAs, as for other RPOs and community groups, should include a defined exit strategy to avoid dependency.

Collective action can be a useful means of empowering people with limited resources. For example, it can help poor producers to meet the costs of participating in markets from which they would otherwise be excluded (see box 3.10 for a description of how collective action has worked in dairy development in India). Experience with many failed

---

Box 3.10 Operation Flood: A Dairy Project Reaches Millions of Poor and Landless People in India

Operation Flood, supported by the World Bank, World Food Program, and other donors from the mid-1970s to the mid-1990s, was developed to promote smallholder dairy production in India. The project started as a marketing project but gradually came to support production and input services as well. It was based on a three-tiered cooperative system comprising:

- village-level dairy cooperative societies, which are controlled by farmers and have an elected management committee that includes at least one woman;
- regional milk producers' unions that own transport equipment and dairy plants for collecting and processing milk; and
- state federations for interstate sales and coordination.

The National Dairy Development Board provided technical support for Operation Flood, which now has 9 million members (60 percent are landless) and processes about 30 million liters of milk each day. The most successful World Bank operation in the livestock sector, Operation Flood has made important contributions to poverty reduction, human health, and nutrition.

Source: de Haan et al. 2001; World Bank internal documents.

cooperatives has shown that meaningful local associations cannot be created from above, but public policy can do a great deal to encourage their development. Policies can provide for training, financial support, the capacity to resolve disputes, and the means to enforce decisions when conflicts emerge within and between groups. Another way to broaden responsibility for development at the local level is community-driven development (CDD), an approach to participatory planning that often provides communities with investment funds (discussed in chapter 4). All of these support systems create an environment in which local associations are likely to flourish.

Institutions for Agricultural Innovation Must Change

Agricultural growth is no longer a matter of finding more land or water to produce crops. Instead, growth will depend on the capacity to innovate. It will rely on science and technology to make the best use of existing resources to raise agricultural productivity and intensify and diversify agricultural production.

Global changes underway in the socioeconomic, political, technological, and environmental landscape will spur an unprecedented demand for agricultural knowledge that cannot be met by the current agricultural R&D systems. *The knowledge needed for rural people to cope with change must come from new sources. It must engage a range of new partners and users more fully to:*

- produce new agricultural technologies to contribute to rapid economic growth worldwide;
- facilitate adjustment to a rapidly changing and highly competitive international economy;
- address environmental concerns; and
- help reduce poverty by increasing the supply of staple products.

In developing countries, most agricultural R&D is still publicly financed. This research tends to focus on commodities of limited global importance (although sometimes of great importance to the poor) or on technologies whose benefits cannot be appropriated, such as methods for managing natural resources. The World Bank has been a leader in supporting public agricultural research at the level of over US$100 million per year over the past decade, together with its annual grant of US$50 million to CGIAR.

Investments in science and technology have proven to be among the most effective instruments for countries to remain competitive in a market economy. Even so, developing countries consistently underinvest in modernizing their

Figure 3.2 Agricultural Research Investment as a Share of Agricultural GDP, Public Sector Only

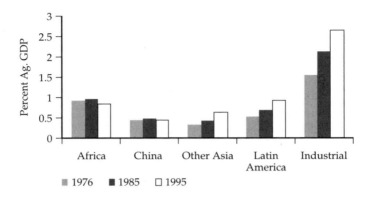

Source: Pardey and Beintema 2001.

innovation systems (figure 3.2), despite the extremely high (though variable) social rate of return on public investment in agricultural R&D (table 3.1) and the impressive impact on poverty reduction (Byerlee and Alex 2002).

Notwithstanding their past successes, public agricultural research institutions have often been rendered ineffective by entrenched bureaucracies, political interference, the inability to retain the best scientists, and poor links with their clients. *The challenge to increase the "knowledge-intensity" of production and reduce poverty will not be met without investments in*

Table 3.1 Estimated Rates of Return to Investment in Agricultural Research (based on studies carried out from 1953 to 1997)

Region	Number of estimates	Median rate of return (%)
Africa	188	34
Asia	222	50
Latin America	262	43
Middle East/North Africa	11	36
All developing countries	683	43
All developed countries	990	46
All	1,772	44

Source: Alston et al. 2000.

agricultural innovation systems that involve a wider range of participants. Public research organizations must increase their collaboration with universities, NGOs, and producer associations. These collaborating organizations must also form strategic alliances with foreign and international public and private research institutions, including the CGIAR centers. Such alliances take advantage of the unique strengths and perspectives of different research institutions and clients, and they will help align research to market trends.

The private sector arguably leads the world in providing new agricultural technologies, primarily technologies that have strong market potential and benefits that private investors can appropriate (e.g., hybrid seed). *Alliances between the public and private sector are especially crucial for harnessing the tools and products of new science, particularly of biotechnology, to benefit the poor (Byerlee and Fischer 2002).* Some important advances have already been made in applying biotechnology for the benefit of small-scale farmers, such as the New Rice for Africa (NERICA) developed through tissue culture and insect-resistant cotton developed through genetic engineering (FAO 2004a). Rapid advances in genomics and related sciences, especially in the private sector, offer the possibility of developing technologies such as drought-tolerant varieties that will sharply reduce the risk and vulnerability of poor farm households struggling with the effects of climate change. The public-private partnerships needed to develop these sorts of technologies will require a new level of engagement and trust between the public and private sector, and they will also require the public sector to master new skills in negotiating intellectual property rights and liability issues.

Public research organizations must also forge closer links with their clients. When R&D involves the end users—groups as diverse as commercial farmers, marginalized farmers, processors, and consumers—the resulting technology is more likely to be useful and used. The institutions for empowerment and decentralization discussed previously are particularly important in fostering the demand-led research and extension that will give producers the knowledge and skills to adapt technology to market opportunities and specific environmental constraints. Innovative approaches have been piloted to put producer organizations firmly in the lead. For example, user funds have been established for producer organizations to match public funds, define adaptive research priorities, and contract with research providers for products and services that meet their specific needs. The local agricultural research committees formed in many Latin American countries provide a successful model for this type of demand-driven research (box 3.11). Latin America has also been a leader in using competitive R&D funding to promote innovative partnerships among public, private, and civil society organizations.

Box 3.11 Multiple Effects of Local Agricultural Research Committees in Latin America

In Colombia, the International Center for Tropical Agriculture (CIAT) (a CGIAR center) supports the development of demand-driven and decentralized research through Local Agricultural Research Committees (CIALs). An impact study that included a survey of 300 households concluded that the CIALs:

- *Strengthened farmer experimentation:* Individual farmers influenced by CIALs were involved in more than 50 kinds of experiments on their own.
- *Improved the quality and relevance of on-farm research:* Seventy-five percent of the CIALs' experimental data could be statistically analyzed by scientists.
- *Developed agro-enterprises:* CIALs have introduced profitable new crops, post-harvest processes and/or new varieties.
- *Improved food security:* Communities with CIALs had fewer respondents who were short of food in the "hungry months" than communities without CIALs.
- *Increased poor people's access to new technologies:* Sixty-three percent of farmers in the poorest strata were adopting between 6 and 15 CIAL technologies, and they were as likely to do so as the better-off strata of farmers. The adoption of new technologies was faster in communities with CIALs and their neighboring communities than in communities that relied on traditional research and extension.

Source: Ashby et al. 2001.

As farmers are increasingly required to engage in more knowledge-intensive agriculture to survive, their need for information and skills will increase exponentially. In extension, as in R&D, public funding is still needed to provide services for small-scale farmers, while the private sector may profitably serve commercial producers. The opportunity to combine agricultural extension with continuing education in business development, marketing, health, and nutrition creates additional benefits to publicly funded extension in poor areas. In many cases, these services can be contracted to the private sector for delivery to users and can be co-financed by the users as well.

The record of donor support for extension systems is mixed. Many of the failures resulted when public sector extension was supported in an unsustainable manner; once the donor organization withdrew, the extension service foundered. Future support for extension systems must be

---

**Box 3.12 Making Extension More Relevant
and Accountable to Users: Experience in
República Bolivariana de Venezuela**

In the early 1990s, República Bolivariana de Venezuela decentralized its
extension system with the objective of empowering local governments and
beneficiaries to select service providers that met their particular needs. The
system clearly defined the functions and responsibilities of the various
actors as well as the links that would facilitate communication among
them all.

The Venezuelan experience highlights the way contracting with exten-
sionists from the private sector, NGOs, and local community organizations
can make the extension system more demand-driven and accountable to
clients. The community associations and NGOs have provided a base for
including different groups, including small-scale farmers and women, and
they have led to the creation of administrative and political organizations
capable of interacting with authorities at the state and national level. It
proved difficult to ensure that beneficiaries would contribute to the extension service, however, and the local capacity to supervise contracts was over-
estimated, underscoring the importance of *carefully phasing in decentralization.*

Source: World Bank internal documents.

---

designed in a way that makes extension accountable to users and funding
sources, promotes gender equity, establishes quality control systems, targets the poor, and promotes environmental conservation. No template
exists for extension services that meet all of these admittedly large
requirements. However, growing evidence suggests that there are significant benefits from establishing decentralized systems that involve the
private sector and civil society and that create incentive systems based
largely on private provision of services (box 3.12). Even so, in most of the
poorer countries, extension services will remain publicly funded because
the conditions are not yet in place for privatization (Anderson and Feder
2004).

Institutions for Supply-Chain Management:
Widening Access to New Markets

*Expanded opportunities for farmers in domestic and foreign markets are increas-
ing the demand for institutions that can help producers compete in global markets and facilitate coordination along the supply chain from farmers to processors
and retailers.* Aside from developing appropriate regulatory institutions

(including systems of grades and standards), support for supply-chain management can involve business development services, trade and producer associations, market information systems, and institutional arrangements for private and public sector cooperation.

The development of an agricultural value chain requires an entrepreneur to see a market opportunity, elicit production from the farm base, process and package the product appropriately, and market the output. The skills required for these activities are usually lacking in developing and transitional economies, partly because of the long dominance of parastatals and partly because of the rapid shift in demand from undifferentiated commodities to branded products. Agribusiness development services have often succeeded in helping small local firms to access new market opportunities when they clearly define the objectives and clientele, recruit competent staff, and separate technical and financial services (see also chapter 4).

Trade associations, community associations, and producer organizations may also have a role in improving coordination among actors in a value chain and in communicating the needs of industry to government, as they did for some 20,000 indigenous farm households in Guatemala (box 3.13). Associations can help organize production, negotiate contracts, improve market information systems, promote products, coordinate research, enforce quality standards, and pool risks. These functions have become increasingly important with the rise of global sourcing and private grades and standards.

A major institutional challenge is to ensure that the poor can participate in these arrangements and capture the benefits from new markets. There can be a significant employment effect from agribusiness, especially for women, and often at higher wages than traditional agriculture can offer (Dolan and Sorby 2003; Minot and Ngigi 2003). There is considerable evidence

---

Box 3.13 Snow Peas Support Indigenous Households in Guatemala

About 20,000 indigenous households in Guatemala succeeded in supplying one-third of the U.S. market for snow peas in the 1990s. Trade and community associations secured funds to establish a distribution system with dozens of intermediaries and over 50 exporters. Through this system, snow peas were packed and shipped within 24 hours of being picked. In 1996, farmers earned an average US$1,400 from very small plots of less than 0.25 hectare.

Source: Gulliver 2001.

of smallholders successfully supplying higher-value crops for international markets and supermarkets, sometimes without public support
(van der Meer 2004). These range from horticulture in Kenya and Zimbabwe to cut flowers in China and Uganda, fish in Bangladesh, and
farmers' organizations supplying supermarkets in Brazil, Argentina, and
Chile.[6] In most of these cases, farmers' associations have been effective
in helping smallholders participate in supply chains through a variety of
contractual arrangements to market their products and to access inputs
at better terms (box 3.14). The World Bank has supported several
schemes to foster small-scale farmers' participation in global supply
chains, especially for higher value products such as shade-grown and
organic coffee in Central America (box 3.15).

Despite these success stories, small-scale farmers' organizations for
high-value exports are still very challenging to scale up and sustain. The
case of the Asumpal farmers' cooperative in Guatemala is a good example.
Farmers received technical assistance, technology, and market access, but

---

Box 3.14 Mali: Building Mango Export Systems

In the 1990s, the Agricultural Trading and Processing Promotion Agency,
an NGO, was established as an autonomous body under the Chamber of
Agriculture through a government agreement. The agency undertook to
design and implement an export promotion project for Malian mangoes.
It specifically sought to restructure supply chains, develop commercialization channels, and promote the application of research and technology.
The agency identified a Côte d'Ivoire enterprise willing to set up a joint
venture and share risks. It has guaranteed a fixed price to the importer,
who bears the logistical and commercial risks associated with exporting
the product. The agency acts as an intermediary between the producer
associations and their trading partners and provides extension services
to growers and pack-house employees to increase productivity, reduce
costs, and improve quality. Producer associations assist with training
and technical assistance, and they work to pool production and negotiate contracts.

Benefits include profitability for all partners, access to new European
markets, reduction by half in transit time to Northern Europe, higher-
quality products delivered to customers, timely payments to growers,
diversified farm incomes, training of the rural labor force, the introduction
of improved technologies, price increases of 25 percent to growers, higher
pack-house employment (60 percent of employees are women), and
improved pack-house working conditions and pay.

Source: World Bank 2004b.

Box 3.15 Smallholders and the
Growing Market for Organic Products

Consumers, especially in developed countries, have been increasingly willing to pay a premium for organic food because they believe it is safer to eat and less harmful to the environment. Organic certification is often regarded as a particularly favorable alternative for smallholders, most of whom already use organic production methods.

The potential of markets for organic products is illustrated by the expanding market share for certified organic bananas to 20 percent in Switzerland and by producer prices for organic bananas in Ecuador that are almost double the price of uncertified bananas. Efforts to improve smallholders' access to these lucrative markets must ensure that marketing systems clearly signal which quality requirements are valued by consumers and incorporate mechanisms to deliver those quality traits.

Even when poor producers organize successfully and supply markets for organic products, not everyone may be able to get on the organic bandwagon. Currently a 20 percent market share seems to be the approximate upper limit of the organic market, as seen with dairy products in Denmark and horticultural products in Germany.

Sources: FAO 2004b; Hellin and Higman 2002.

---

they left the market because they could not sustain the quality of the produce, supply it regularly, or resolve conflicts over side-selling (Dugger 2004). In Kenya and Zimbabwe, smallholders grew nearly 75 percent of fruits and vegetables in 1992, but by 1998 four of the largest exporters were sourcing only 18 percent of produce from smallholders (Dolan and Humphrey 2000). Where markets are not competitive, contract farming and vertical integration (in which the same entity controls some or all of the steps in the supply chain, e.g., from the seed and other inputs used to grow a crop to the processing and sale of the final product) threaten to make farmers overly dependent on one integrator.

The experiences of many producer organizations that successfully participated in these markets have demonstrated the importance of keeping the private sector in the driver's seat; otherwise private entities will not invest. Public support remains critical, however, for establishing a conducive legal, regulatory, and policy framework (e.g., contract law and grades and standards); promoting the organization of small-scale producers with good leadership and understanding of market requirements; and helping to provide training, technology, and quality control systems.

Financial Institutions to Serve the Poor
and Develop Private Enterprise

Access to a complete range of financial services would greatly facilitate rural and agricultural development. Throughout the developing world, liquidity constraints prohibit smallholders from intensifying production and stifle the growth of small agro-based enterprises. Reliable and sustainable access to short- and medium-term credit is essential for farmers and processors to adapt and update production systems, obtain working capital to meet seasonal requirements, and benefit from emerging opportunities in the food supply chain. In addition, reliable payment systems to transfer funds within the supply chain, deposit facilities to safeguard cash and working capital, and possibly insurance services are required.

The profitable development of financial institutions in rural areas is inhibited by high transactions costs and default risks resulting from:

- low population density;
- poor physical infrastructure;
- the simultaneous vulnerability of many farmers to a specific price or yield risk;
- the small sizes and volumes of transactions;
- the lack of easily marketable collateral;
- an unfavorable legal framework concerning property and collateral rights should bankruptcy occur or contracts prove difficult to enforce; and
- a generally unfavorable business environment and lack of profitability.

Informal systems such as rotating savings and credit associations and moneylenders provide some financial services with relatively low transactions costs, but these systems are limited by their small scale, short geographic reach, narrow range of instruments, and narrow focus. Directed credit schemes and subsidized credit offered through state-owned institutions have yielded only modest effects on development while incurring high fiscal costs and discouraging the formation of strong, private financial institutions.

The financial systems approach seeks to overcome the deficiencies of past approaches by treating rural finance as part of a wider process of developing financial markets. It emphasizes the need for sustainable financial institutions that provide services tailored to the distinct conditions of people from a range of social strata, who engage in different economic activities. These services are designed to include groups who previously had no access to them, such as illiterate people (box 3.16).

Box 3.16 Rural People Demand
a Range of Financial Services

- *Savings:* Opportunities for financial savings so that farmers do not
  have to store wealth in low-yielding and risky physical stocks (including livestock).
- *Short-term finance:* Seasonal working capital available according to
  agricultural calendars enables farmers to purchase inputs and intensify
  production.
- *Term finance:* Loans and leases for a year or longer improve access to
  farm machinery, irrigation equipment, land improvements, livestock,
  tree crops, and processing equipment.
- *Leasing:* Lease agreements provide access to equipment while ownership remains with the lending institution. Producers can avoid the
  effects of an unfavorable legal framework, and transactions costs are
  generally lower.
- *Low-cost money transfer for remittances:* Income from national or
  international remittances is important in most developing economies,
  disproportionately so in many poor rural areas where it may be the
  principal source of income.
- *Insurance:* Insurance products demanded in rural areas span crop and
  livestock insurance, health and life insurance, and forward contracts
  such as warehouse receipt systems.

Source: Authors.

---

*Rather than pushing specific credit lines, efforts to strengthen financial sys-
tems either strengthen viable financial institutions or create the conditions under
which they can emerge.* The capacity of financial institutions to serve agriculture can be enhanced by developing a profitable agricultural sector,
providing a favorable legal framework and technical assistance for institutional development, and building capacity for financial institutions to
install efficient internal processing and management information systems
that reduce transactions costs and increase the quality of their portfolios.

The development of lasting financial institutions can also be encouraged by promoting deposit insurance to attract local funds and creating
financial sector infrastructure such as credit information bureaus and
bank training institutes. Financial institutions must also have the ability
to charge interest rates that cover risks and nonperforming loans. Nonin-
terference by government policies and politicians in credit decisions,
responsible accounting practices, and transparency of decision making
are other cornerstones for developing sustainable financial institutions. In

rural areas, policies that establish well-defined property rights and access to efficient communications infrastructure are the key to directly reducing financial institutions' transactions costs, increasing the quality of their portfolios, and thus supporting an expanding and diversifying clientele.

In recent years, innovative microfinance institutions (MFIs) have helped rural groups, particularly the poor and women, to expand their productive activities. Although serving markets not covered by traditional financial institutions, MFIs have been most successful in high-potential areas. They have been slow to spread into less densely populated and poorer rural areas where transactions costs are higher and income sources less diversified. Some MFIs have facilitated procedures for agricultural loans by adapting disbursement and repayment to agricultural production cycles, applying more flexible collateral requirements, targeting services to diversified agricultural borrowers to mitigate risk, and selecting their locations strategically. Innovative MFIs have been piloted in Kenya, where rural areas are reached through mobile banking, loans to farmers are secured by contracts with agribusiness companies, and a donor agency has supported institutional capacity building (box 3.17).

Box 3.17 Kenya's Equity Building Society: Bringing Banking Services Directly to Rural Customers

The Equity Building Society (EBS) provides more than 250,000 low- and moderate-income citizens in Nairobi and in high-potential Central Province with microfinance services through a network of branch offices and mobile banking units. After a decade of extending long-term mortgage loans to an untargeted clientele with feeble results, EBS altered its approach. It began tailoring loan and savings products for the microfinance market, eventually adding two agricultural loan products secured by tea and dairy farmers' contracts with processing and marketing companies. According to DFID estimates, as of early 2004, EBS's mobile units profitably served 29 villages and had achieved 36 percent market penetration in the areas served, which constituted about 12,000 clients on a regular basis (47 percent were women).

EBS's mobile banking operations have also been successful, covering their costs and accounting for more than 1.3 million in deposits in 2003. Moreover, mobile banking has decreased branch congestion and improved the image and visibility of EBS as a supplier of financial services to the people.

Source: CGAP 2004.

Aside from MFIs, numerous institutions that are active in rural finance could be strengthened, including state-owned agricultural banks and privately owned commercial banks in rural areas, postal and savings banks, cooperative financial institutions, leasing companies, processors, traders, input dealers, and informal financial intermediaries such as rotating savings and credit associations. Still other arrangements could be initiated to provide financial services, including community-based, locally run microfinance institutions that collaborate with state agricultural banks to provide individual loans (box 3.18). Some additional innovative approaches to agricultural finance include index-based crop and livestock insurance systems (see below) and credit based on warehouse receipts to facilitate private storage. These approaches are being pilot tested; it is not yet clear whether successful efforts can be scaled up.

Box 3.18 Mali: Self-Managed Village Savings and Credit Banks Assist the Rural Poor

The experience of the Self-Managed Village Savings and Credit Banks (CVECA) network in Niono demonstrates the potential of transforming an unsuccessful state agricultural group-lending program into a decentralized, community-led provider of individual credit. CVECA was modeled after two successful networks in the Dogon and First Region zones of Mali with assistance from the International Center for Development Banks (CIDR). Comprised of 51 decentralized, locally run banks, the Niono network drew on members' savings deposits and loans from the National Agricultural Development Bank to award US$2.4 million in credit in 2002, with an average loan size of US$233. Most of these loans were for agriculture—especially rice cultivation. Over three years, from 2000 through 2002, operating in an impoverished rural zone, the Niono network provided an average of US$2 million in credit annually through more than 9,000 loans. It accomplished this in an apparently sustainable manner, earning enough revenues to cover its operations almost twice over where the banks have established a strong base, and achieving mostly positive financial growth.

   The CVECA case illustrates the importance of a decentralized and largely autonomous operation; long-term donor and investor commitment for both financial and technical support; an independent service to provide financial monitoring and technical assistance; and a well-structured partnership between a state agricultural development institution and a network of small, village-run banks that capitalized on the stable liquidity of the former and the grassroots penetration and adaptability of the latter.

Source: CGAP 2004.

Sustainable financial institutions are often slowest to appear in marginal, sparsely populated areas where poverty is most extreme and the liquidity constraint is most binding. *While the long-term goal should be to develop financially independent and sustainable institutions, the immediate need for financial services in marginal areas implies a role for the public sector to motivate the development of institutions and to build capacity.* Subsidies to institutions for start-up operating expenses and matching grants to develop capacity can be appropriate in areas where commercial banking services are unavailable. Guarantee schemes may facilitate the delivery of financial services where commercial institutions exist, but they are deterred by the risk involved in agricultural lending. Such schemes need to be designed in strict accordance with best practices to avoid the risks of moral hazard and high transaction costs that have historically plagued guarantee arrangements. Where commercial opportunities are greater, public assistance to provide the poor with business development services and financial management training can widen access to existing financial institutions. In either case, the public role should be to provide limited-term support to create the conditions under which financial institutions can grow.

Risk Management Institutions to Cope with New Market Realities

In liberalized markets, the risk of fluctuating prices for inputs and outputs has shifted from governments to producers and consumers. The concurrent expansion of farming populations into more marginal areas has increased the number of farmers facing severe drought and other climatic shocks. Other sources of risk for farmers include crop damage from fire or livestock, pest and disease outbreaks, loss of labor through illness or death, loss of land caused by badly designed titling schemes, and failures of transportation or irrigation infrastructure. The poor are at the greatest risk, since they often cannot use either formal or customary institutions to protect themselves. The lack of institutions to help the poor cope with risk makes it particularly difficult for food-insecure households to attempt most agricultural innovations, with the result that they are locked into relatively less productive farming activities.

Farmers and firms have "traditional" means of managing their risks through savings, diversification, share tenancy contracts, community-based relationships of reciprocity, and selective market relationships, but these risk management methods may reduce investment and average returns. They are also frequently ineffective at helping communities deal with risks that are likely to affect everyone at the same time, such as the risk of drought.

The move toward liberalized markets requires attention to institutions that support improved risk management more directly. Many efforts have been made to extend the reach of rural risk markets in developing economies, but the conditions that encourage effective risk management must be present. In principle, a well-functioning financial system serving rural areas is the single most important condition for effective risk management. A stable policy climate, product diversification, market development, irrigation, strong producer organizations, information (including market and weather information systems), and better physical and institutional infrastructure all reduce risk or increase the capacity to manage it. Experience has shown that initiatives to meet these general needs can have large payoffs in many risky pastoral systems (box 3.19).

Small farms and other small businesses in developing countries rarely use market-based instruments such as insurance to manage risk, because they lack insurable assets and there are no agricultural risk markets. Now, however, opportunities are emerging to engage in such markets. To address risk from changes in global prices, the public sector can facilitate the use of existing commodity exchanges (including spot markets) as well as more complex markets for risk management and insurance. In Mexico, cotton growers hedge their price risk by participating in a voluntary government program that guarantees a minimum cotton price fixed using the New York Cotton

---

Box 3.19 Pastoralists Manage Extreme Environmental Risk in Kenya and Mongolia

In many areas, risk may be best addressed by focusing on underlying causes rather than simply establishing insurance institutions. Pastoralists in Kenya's arid districts cope with a fragile physical environment, poor and variable water resources, and recurrent droughts that can cause catastrophic livestock losses. The Arid Lands Resource Management Project builds pastoralists' capacity to deal with risk through (1) programs to provide early warnings of drought, mitigate its impact, and speed recovery; (2) infrastructure development to improve livestock marketing; and (3) community development to increase the capacity to deal with drought.

Like their Kenyan counterparts, pastoralists in Mongolia cope with extreme environmental risk. The Mongolia Sustainable Livelihoods Project aims to reduce vulnerability and promote security and sustainability through community-driven programs to diversify incomes, manage pastures, forecast risk, monitor weather trends, and develop an early warning system. A livestock insurance scheme based on a risk index is being developed.

Source: World Bank 2004b.

Box 3.20 A Tanzanian Coffee Cooperative Wakes Up to Ways of Hedging Its Price Risk

One of the largest coffee cooperatives in Tanzania historically paid a minimum price to members for their coffee at delivery and provided subsequent payments depending on sales and market performance. While the guaranteed first payment gives farmers a form of price stability, it can be disastrous for the cooperative. If the cooperative guarantees a low first payment at the beginning of the season and the market price rises, farmers will sell to traders who pay the full market price, but if the cooperative guarantees a high first payment at the beginning of the season and the market price falls, the cooperative stands to lose.

The World Bank began working with the cooperative to strengthen its operations by protecting its prices with market-based hedging instruments. The cooperative designed a hedging strategy that matched its risk profile, using the options in the international market to provide a floor price to protect against declining prices. Only after they had scrutinized the management and financial viability of the cooperative did insurance providers approve it as a new client and enable it to enter the market to hedge its price risk. Technical assistance and training helped insurance providers build confidence in the credibility of the cooperative as a client and build the awareness and technical capacity of cooperative members. Although the approach is promising, the transaction costs remain high, and the sustainability of this scheme remains uncertain.

Source: World Bank 2004b.

Futures Exchange. The World Bank has helped Tanzanian coffee producers to reduce price risks using international derivative markets (box 3.20), but this approach may not be sustainable in this case, owing to the high cost of the small number of transactions and the lack of replication among other cooperatives.

Compared with schemes for price insurance, schemes for crop and livestock insurance face very different problems. Government agricultural insurance programs have often collapsed because of their high administrative costs, opportunistic behavior on the part of the insured, unequal access to information by everyone involved, and systemic risk (e.g., the likelihood that nearly all participants would suffer from the same disastrous event, such as a crop disease epidemic). A more effective role for the government would be to improve the quality and accessibility of private

insurance by providing the enabling environment for rural financial institutions, supporting information services and technologies, and providing
physical infrastructure, effective regulations, and contract dispute mechanisms. Pilot experiences with weather-based insurance show that with
appropriate facilitation and technical assistance, the private sector can
deliver crop insurance (box 3.21).

A key factor in determining demand for weather-risk hedges is credit,
which often requires insurance. Those in need of credit will often be intermediaries such as agricultural banks or insurance companies, or input

---

Box 3.21 Insurance Protects Producers
from Drought in India

A World Bank–assisted pilot project helped to launch India's first rainfall
insurance program. The project demonstrated that weather-indexed insurance could benefit farmers and could avoid the problems of moral hazard
and high administrative costs associated with traditional crop insurance
programs. Under the project, a local bank sold policies to producers, with
the premium and maximum liability varying by scale. For example, farms
between 0.8 and 2 hectares paid Rs 600 with a maximum liability of Rs
20,000. The payout structure was based on rainfall. It weighted rainfall
deficiencies in the more critical periods for plant growth more heavily
than deficiencies in other periods.

Following the pilot project, one of India's largest microfinance institutions began to offer rainfall insurance. The local bank offers policies to its
borrowers as well as to outside clients, such as members of women's self-
help groups, and it hopes to lower the interest rate for borrowers based on
the reduced risk of default. Lessons include:

- The index must be based on long-term statistical information and
  credible actuarial models. To this end, the public sector can develop
  information sources such as risk maps.
- The trigger (the event or circumstance that permits the policy holder to
  claim payment) must be an unambiguous threshold of a quantifiable
  variable over which farmers have no control.
- The payment schedule must be clear, quantifiable, and monitored by
  an independent third party.
- Education programs and technical assistance for stakeholders should
  be provided.
- Combining index-based programs with other types of insurance and
  financial services can improve the effectiveness of the trigger.

Source: Hess 2003.

suppliers and agro-processing companies exposed to volume risk, especially where crop insurance to individual farmers fails due to high expense ratios. Ultimately, a vibrant weather-indexed insurance market will emerge if it is supported by effective local advocates who have learned about successful experiences in emerging markets, and if global insurers are willing to shoulder some immediate costs to reap the longer-term benefits of a globally diversified weather-risk market.

The roles of the public and private sector in efforts to manage risk must be carefully balanced. Governments have responsibility for some direct involvement in managing severe catastrophic risks, as the private sector will not become involved. Until the public sector can accommodate catastrophic risks (e.g., a drought that occurs once in 50 years), the private sector will not provide services for more frequent events where probabilities are better known. Public support in managing risk for major catastrophic events includes safety nets, cash transfer programs to help people cope with disaster, postdisaster rehabilitation, and sometimes a guaranteed payment when major disasters strike. For example, the proposed Mongolia Livestock Insurance Scheme (box 3.19) would include a government payment if livestock mortality exceeds 40 percent. To avoid moral hazards, these programs should be transparent. Payouts must be based on an unambiguous threshold of a variable over which farmers have no control, which is quantifiable, and which is determined by an independent and credible third party.

In conclusion, new strategies for managing the negative consequences of volatile rural incomes rely more heavily on markets to supplement the many ways in which governments and households manage risks. Key questions still remain concerning the roles and links for formal, informal, private, and public insurance markets and how to use public-private partnerships to share or lessen the high costs of bringing these markets to small-scale farmers. Issues include the extent to which informal risk-sharing systems benefit from formal insurance markets, the value of publicly provided catastrophe insurance, the capacity of governments to meet those obligations under all circumstances, and what components of price and yield risk should fall to individuals, governments, and donors (Larson, Anderson, and Varangis 2004).

Secure and Tradable Rights to Land and Water Have Multiple Benefits

When rights to land and water are poorly defined, rural people have very insecure control over their assets. Unclear property rights spark conflict, promote resource degradation, and discourage investment. They have a disproportionate impact on the poorest of the poor, who rely most on communal or open-access resources. Well-defined, secure, and transferable property rights are also a prerequisite for efficient land and water markets.

In Honduras, for instance, land markets using formal land titles and record systems have given smallholders incentives to improve productivity and manage natural resources more sustainably, have facilitated access to credit and other services, have allowed farmers to engage temporarily in off-farm employment, and have facilitated land transfers and efficient land use (a transaction effect). According to López (1996), these combined outcomes provided an annual rate of return on the cost of land titling of 17 percent. This is just one example of how secure land rights can promote agricultural development that benefits the poor.

In general, a good land policy will include:

- a strong land administration component that establishes land rights and the complementary mechanisms of titling, registration, transfer, dispute resolution, and revenue collection, in addition to supporting the development of land markets; and
- a land reform component in areas where injustices have led to inefficient or highly inequitable land distribution.

Titling and registration processes must be defined and implemented to improve the security of land tenure and ensure that the claims of smallholders and marginalized groups, including women, receive equal protection under the law. This goal extends beyond simply issuing land titles to poor farmers and women, however. A land administration policy in Laos successfully conferred property rights on women (box 3.22).

In itself, secure land tenure yields important benefits to the rural poor, but more complete land administration systems are needed for cost-efficient land transfer and application of property taxes. In some contexts, formal or legal recognition of informal land rights systems and customary tenure arrangements may be all that is required. By devolving land administration to state, local, and district offices that operate within a consistent national framework, it is possible to increase the system's efficiency, cost-effectiveness, transparency, and social equity. Where the public sector has only limited capacity, the involvement of local community groups and the private sector (for example, through contracting out surveying and mapping) can greatly facilitate the implementation of land administration. There is also a need to strengthen land rental markets by providing a legal framework for long-term leasing arrangements, enforcing rental contracts, reducing transactions costs, and simplifying contractual mechanisms.

Box 3.22 Laos: Land Titling Yields Results for Women and Men

For land titling to serve the poor, it must be based on an appropriate legal framework and be sensitive to the requirements of vulnerable groups. In the Lao People's Democratic Republic, a titling program first built a legislative basis for land administration. A cabinet-level committee was mandated to identify key policy issues and develop corresponding decrees. With interim ministerial regulations for adjudication and registration in place, pilot projects could issue titles in advance of final legislation. Lessons from pilot projects were then integrated into more substantive legal reforms. The project made a conscious effort to ensure that the formalization of land tenure strengthened the rights of women, who had been excluded from earlier titling efforts owing to their social status, workloads, and low literacy rates. Under the project, 34 percent of titles were issued to women, 38 percent were issued jointly (typically to married couples), and 24 percent went to men alone.

Source: Authors.

As there is generally an inverse relationship between farm size and productivity, redistributing land in a way that favors smallholders can provide both efficiency and equity benefits in situations where land distribution has been highly inequitable. It is important to emphasize, however, that conventional land reform programs, which have been limited only to the transfer of land with no allowance for complementary investment, technical assistance, and supplementary resources, generally have not achieved their objectives of equity and efficiency. For example, imperfect credit markets and insecure property rights in Nicaragua and the Philippines complicated the use of land as collateral, and poor access to market opportunities caused the beneficiaries of land reform to sell their land, often at prices well below its productive value (Jonakin 1996).

New voluntary land reform approaches (often called "market-assisted" or "negotiated" programs) have been piloted in Brazil using government grants. These approaches allow beneficiaries to choose the type of productive enterprise in which they will engage, identify land, and arrange for the necessary investments and technical support. Land redistribution through such market-based approaches usually requires substantial external financing for land purchases and technical assistance. Even with external financing, land transfers may require compulsory acquisition, and redistribution may fail to serve the targeted populations. To date, there are no rigorous quantitative evaluations that compare market-assisted land reform with other redistributive reforms (e.g., in terms of costs to the public budget). Even so, some models for land redistribution show promise, including community-managed, market-assisted land reform programs in Brazil, which receive strong support from local governments and NGOs.

Like land, water is a critical resource that is often managed by administrative mechanisms, leading to inefficient and inequitable allocation and use. Incentive structures may not exist or are distorted. Service providers may have little incentive or accountability for quality service, and farmers—faced with subsidies and institutional inflexibility—also have few incentives to manage water more efficiently. Water subsidies are not only inefficient but also generally inequitable (World Bank 2003f, 2004c).

Charging for water is a political issue, and it is difficult to get the price right. In many cases, user fees cover the costs of operating and maintaining the infrastructure, but this price is well below water's scarcity value in agricultural or nonfarm uses. Further research is needed on how to design a successful incentive system that can take stakeholders' varied interests into account, introduce change gradually, and provide complementary investments and innovations to increase farm productivity.

The long-term goal for managing water resources should be a market-based system that allocates water through tradable water rights. Property rights over irrigation water are seldom well defined and transferred in markets. These problems are compounded in areas where irrigation relies on extracting groundwater reserves. By establishing tradable water use rights, represented by entitlements, and providing an administrative system in which trading can occur, governments can give rights holders (usually in the agricultural sector) the economic incentives to use their entitlements and water supplies efficiently. During shortages and periods of changes in demand, high-priority users can compete in the market for water, and those who voluntarily give up their entitlement are compensated at a rate determined by the market value. In theory, this system encourages investment in more efficient irrigation technology, promotes water conservation, reallocates water to higher value uses, and enhances agricultural incomes. Although evidence in support of this system was seen in the pioneer Chilean water markets (box 3.23), more recent studies indicate that the rigid legal and regulatory framework for water markets is increasing problems in river basin management, water conflicts, and environmental protection (Bauer 2004).

To date, only a handful of countries have active tradable water rights systems, because they are complex and costly. *Pilot cases of market-based transfer mechanisms highlight the fact that the process is evolutionary and may*

Box 3.23 Chile: Water Rights Encourage Diversification and Reduce Poverty

Tradable water rights were established in Chile during land market reforms in 1975, when land that had been collectivized in 1966 was privatized. Former landowners received 40 percent of their original land along with the proportional right to water historically used on this land. The remaining 60 percent of the land and the water rights were allocated to former workers on the land. These reforms, along with broader economic reforms such as trade and exchange rate liberalization, led to the creation of water markets in the early 1980s, raised water use efficiency, and promoted rapid crop diversification. Water market reform also increased the scarcity value of water and fostered a large increase in area planted with fruits and vegetables, which require less water per gross value of output than field crops. Aggregate water use efficiency in agriculture increased by an estimated 22–26 percent between 1976 and 1992 (Frias 1992).

Because of the intensive use of labor in processing fruits and vegetables, particularly for the export market, agricultural diversification has substantially reduced rural poverty. Using data from 1990 to 1996, López and Anriquez (2003) estimated that a 4.5 percent increase in agricultural output in Chile led to an 8–11 percent decrease in the poverty headcount, mainly by raising real wages of unskilled workers.

Sources: Frias 1992; Munita 1994; Rosegrant, Schleyer, and Yadav 1995; World Bank, 2004c.

---

take many years to adopt. This means that a flexible enabling legal framework of entitlement and transfer must be coupled with strong, long-term capacity building and technical support. Many countries have made private water markets a long-term policy goal and are implementing more immediate reforms based on incentive systems, including the establishment of water charging systems and the strengthening of WUAs to sustain the maintenance and administration of irrigation systems. Additional research is needed to provide information about how private water markets currently work and about mechanisms for handling externalities and water conflicts to scale up the development of water markets.

Environmental Policies and Institutions

In many cases, markets do not fully account for the social and environmental costs and benefits of agricultural activities, and corrective measures may be needed. For example, unregulated applications of chemical pesticides and fertilizers can lead to excessive water contamination and health hazards. In many countries, regulations to limit such externalities do in fact exist, but they are rarely enforced. So-called green taxes (e.g., a tax on pesticides) can be used to discourage the use of inputs with negative environmental effects. Although these policies may be difficult to implement, a first step in avoiding negative externalities in many situations is to remove the subsidies that promote them.

Agriculture also produces many positive externalities that merit public sector support. Conservation tillage technologies can, for example, preserve or enhance biodiversity and help mitigate the effects of global warming by sequestering carbon. Where extensive land use drives habitat loss, threatens biodiversity, and causes carbon emissions, there are important environmental benefits when farmers intensify production rather than cultivate new land. Support could consist of infrastructure development in areas already under cultivation or incentives to implement resource-conserving technologies such as watershed programs, although the sustainability of such schemes remains uncertain. Taxes on industries that benefit from biodiversity, like tourism, or on polluters, such as automotive industries, could be levied to cover green payments to farmers who adopt techniques that preserve biodiversity and sequester carbon. For example, the government of Costa Rica has introduced a gasoline tax that supports reforestation and agro-forestry, which are promoted in the project described in box 3.3.

Other Regulatory Instruments

Regulations provide a framework that guides the behavior of individuals and organizations; reduces the uncertainty of decision making; and protects consumers, workers, and the natural environment (box 3.24). Robust private investment requires a legal environment that establishes the sanctity of contracts, clearly defines property rights, resolves disputes impartially, and provides safeguards against collusive or monopolistic behavior. Business regulations in many developing countries escalate the costs of private sector operations and open avenues for corruption. More effective and streamlined regulations can allow greater private sector activity by lowering transactions costs, reducing the risk associated with doing business, and improving the marketability of products.

Product certification and safety regulations: Businesses and consumers benefit from enforced standards for agricultural products that simultaneously protect health and welfare and reduce the costs of doing business. Verifying and certifying seeds and plant propagation materials and regulating agrochemicals can be critical for intensification and cannot be left to the private sector alone. Yet regulatory and testing requirements for

---

**Box 3.24 Roles of Regulation for Economic
and Social Well-Being**

Regulation to improve efficiency of markets includes the provision of:

- contract enforcement and dispute adjudication;
- product grades and standards;
- regulation of market power and collusion; and
- specification of property rights.

Regulation for social protection includes:

- food safety standards;
- natural resource and environmental protection; and
- labor safety and health standards.

Source: Authors.

---

imports of seed and chemicals often have restricted farmers' choices. Effectively enforced, regulations can reduce uncertainty, but they must also be flexible enough to allow farmers to benefit from new technologies or respond to new market opportunities. A shift to regional certification institutions would be one way of accelerating the flow of technology. It would improve on the current practice of repeating lengthy national testing procedures, which are often superfluous because they have been done in a neighboring country under similar conditions.

Inspection and verification services that issue sanitary and phytosanitary certificates are important for protecting environmental quality, ensuring food safety, and accessing foreign markets. Effective food safety institutions protect consumers and reduce transactions costs in the market by removing uncertainty about quality. In many cases an adaptive system of standards, with one set of food safety standards appropriate for local conditions and a second set for export products, may be more suitable than uniform standards (see chapter 2), although such an adaptive system is not recommended by WTO and other international standard-setting organizations.

Biosafety and environmental regulations: Advances in biotechnology present a heightened need for regulation to ensure that the products of biotechnology do not impose large external costs or adversely affect market access. Biosafety regulations must ensure the protection of human and environmental health from the potentially adverse effects of genetically modified organisms, but they should not aim to discourage technical innovation. Their primary objective is to encourage the socially and environmentally desirable use of biological resources.

Aside from biosafety regulations, other central government policies and institutions may be needed to protect natural resources. In many cases, local management of natural resources is inappropriate, either because environmental effects extend beyond the local level or because local resource use is highly contentious and politicized. Because environmental ministries (like agricultural ministries) are generally weak and more focused on preservation than on promoting sustainable agricultural practices, it remains a major challenge to bring agriculture and environment decision makers together.

Entry Points for National Public Policy and Institution Building

At the national level, trade and market reforms must be implemented more broadly and deeply in agriculture, because they are critical for growth as well as for poverty reduction. These reforms must be designed with a careful eye for the many country-specific circumstances that can influence success, including the characteristics and conditions of each country and commodity and the particular impacts on the poor. The need for phasing and sequencing market liberalization has become abundantly clear. Good analytical work is essential to design the appropriate sequence of reforms, establish policies that create safety nets for vulnerable groups, and ensure that the reform process is politically sustainable. Development policy lending, such as Poverty Reduction Support Credit (PRSC), based on sound poverty and social impact assessments, can support safeguards for the poor during the transition.

It is essential to work with national governments, particularly with ministries of agriculture and other local stakeholders, to design adequate links between agricultural reforms that benefit the poor and overall macroeconomic development. National agricultural and rural development strategies are key tools for developing a common vision and consistency of purpose across the sector and among major stakeholders; defining the main policies, institutions, and investments; determining their priority and sequencing; and establishing implementation and monitoring arrangements. Strategies also serve to focus and coordinate donor and government activities for the greatest impact. Support for the preparation of national agricultural and rural development strategies is one of the key action points of the World Bank's rural strategy, *Reaching the Rural Poor*. Much analytical work by the World Bank, especially on sequencing and safety nets, can be an important input into these strategies.

There are many entry points for facilitating small-scale farmers' participation in global supply chains. For example, international donors (USAID in particular) have supported several projects designed to establish or strengthen farmer-led associations. The World Bank, although a relative newcomer in the area of supply chain management, has initiated major analytical work on the costs and benefits of compliance with sanitary and phytosanitary standards and priority investments in managing the supply chain to benefit the poor (World Bank 2005c). Facilities now exist in the World Bank and WTO for mainstreaming SPS needs in economic policy studies and investments. Knowledge gained from this work, together with partnerships with the International Finance Corporation (IFC), NGOs, and producer organizations, and close collaboration with the international standard setting organizations (Codex Alimentarius, Office International des Épizooties, and the International Plant Protection Convention—and technical agencies such as FAO and the World Health Organization) can underpin expanded work in this area.

There is sufficient experience to scale up many kinds of institutional development. These include environmental policies (e.g., paying for environmental services), land and water rights (e.g., land administration, water pricing policies), the development of innovation systems, and irrigation management through WUAs. The World Bank can play a particularly significant role here. As the world's most important donor for public national and international agricultural research, it can support the production of new products to accelerate diversification and market development for small-scale farmers. Scaling up can be done through traditional sector investment lending as well as through new instruments (e.g., programmatic lending) and new partnerships emerging with the IFC (see chapter 6).

For rural finance, the financial systems approach seeks to overcome the deficiencies of past approaches by treating rural finance as part of a wider process of developing financial markets. The multisector capacity of the World Bank provides a comparative advantage in addressing the entire financial system, which is preferred to sector-specific approaches. New models seek to combine financial services with risk management instruments, but these require much more piloting and evaluation, as proven instruments for working effectively with the private sector are still lacking.

Finally, more effective and streamlined regulations can help the private sector to become more active by lowering transactions costs, reducing the risk associated with doing business, and improving the marketability of products.

4

Public Investments for Pro-Poor Growth

In this chapter

Investments in core public goods (e.g., infrastructure, education, and natural resources) have high payoffs in the form of economic growth and reduced poverty. Other types of public investment help to overcome "temporary" market failures, develop markets, and enable the private sector to fully promote economic growth.

What can be done to promote more effective public investments?

- A more balanced approach to agricultural investments can be taken, based on an improved understanding of the distribution of responsibilities between public and private enterprises and civil society.
- A larger share of public expenditures should be allocated to the agricultural sector, especially in Africa, but first current resources must be managed more effectively by shifting resources from private goods and subsidies.
- Through a variety of new public-private co-financing arrangements, the public sector can leverage private investments and strengthen the market orientation of its investments. Time-limited matching grants to the private sector and communities are becoming a particularly popular mechanism for stimulating market development as well as providing assets to smallholders (e.g., through grants for agricultural innovation, business development services, and community-driven development).

Key tasks for the future include:

- Scaling up investments in physical, human, natural, and social capital based on the considerable body of successful experience in the international community.
- Engaging in public expenditure reviews for the agricultural sector to ensure that donor funding is channeled effectively to agriculture through direct budgetary support.
- Refining and expanding approaches for working with the private sector and for matching grant systems that benefit the poor without leading to distortions in the wider economy.

This chapter continues the discussion of the three keys to broad-based agricultural development by describing how public investments can fuel private investment and economic growth in ways that benefit the poor. Growth requires a range of investments—public investment in public goods, private investment in profit-generating private goods, and combined public and private investment in a wide range of goods that have some public as well as private characteristics.

Higher and more effective public investments in agriculture will be required in most countries to meet the MDGs, especially the goals concerned with halving poverty and hunger (Rosegrant et al. 2001). These investments must support core public goods related to infrastructure, agricultural R&D, information, and skills to create an environment that favors private investment. The public sector also may be called upon to make investments over limited time periods to stimulate the private provision of goods and services that are initially too costly or risky for the private sector to provide on its own. Such investments to overcome market failures in agriculture are often best implemented through joint public-private financing and/or delivery. In all cases, the public investment must generate net benefits to society, and the risks of government failure should be less than the risks of market failure.

The Rationale for Public Sector Investment

Compared with their counterparts in other economic sectors in developing countries, agricultural producers and processors face a host of market failures that can justify interventions by the public sector. Market failures can have many sources, including:

- *Externalities:* Externalities are often described as side effects of economic activity (i.e., costs or benefits that affect third parties and not simply those directly involved in an activity). In watershed management, for example, land management by farmers located upstream affects the volume and quality of water available to farmers downstream.
- *Economies of scale:* New enterprises that have a low volume of production often have higher costs and find it more challenging to comply with regulations and standards, such as food safety and quality standards, until they increase in size.
- *Asymmetric information:* All parties in an economic transaction or relationship may not have the same information (for example, small-scale farmers may have virtually no information about a market in which they are trying to compete).
- *Nonexcludability of users:* If anyone can freely obtain and use new knowledge, especially in the form of new technology (such as a new

water conservation practice), there is little impetus for the private sector to develop or provide it.

These market failures can be overcome through regulation and investments in public goods—in economic terms, goods that are largely nonexcludable (potential users cannot be excluded from use by the owners) and nonrival (the consumption of a good does not decrease its use by another) (figure 4.1). Because many goods have only some degree of excludability and rivalry, there is a large intermediate area between pure public and pure private goods, so-called impure public goods. There is considerable potential for the private and public sectors to share responsibility for funding and delivering goods and services that fall into this intermediate area. Table 4.1 illustrates these distinctions for various types of animal health services.

Investments in agricultural research, education, and rural infrastructure are often the most effective in promoting agricultural growth and reducing poverty, though a significant amount of time may pass between the initial investment and its visible impact (see table 4.2). Even in less favorable agricultural areas, public investment can lead to high returns for the poor, as seen in India (Fan, Hazell, and Thorat 1999). Because public resources are so critical to stimulating growth that benefits the poor, they must be targeted carefully to investments that (1) will stimulate private investment and market development, (2) have the maximum effects on productivity growth and the profitability of the private sector, and (3) favor the poor. All of these investment goals are discussed in the sections that follow, along with the benefits and drawbacks of alternative strategies for achieving them.

Figure 4.1 Characteristics and Types of Economic Goods

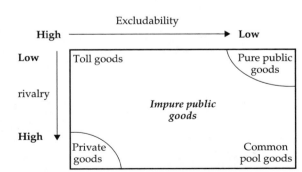

Source: Adapted from van der Meer 2002.

Table 4.1 Economic Characteristics and Delivery of Animal Health Services

	Type of economic good		Type of delivery	
Service	Public	Private	Public	Private
Clinical diagnosis		Private but some consumption externalities		YY
Clinical treatment		Pure private		YY
Vaccine production		Pure private		YY
Vaccination, major contagious diseases	Public because of strong consumption externalities		Y	YY (contracted by public sector)
Vaccination against minor diseases		Private but some consumption externalities		YY
Veterinary surveillance (quarantine, epidemiology)	Public because of strong consumption externalities		Y	Y (contracted by public sector)
Control of veterinary pharmaceutical sales	Public because of moral hazard		Y	Y (contracted by public sector)
Food safety control (meat inspections)	Public because of moral hazard		Y	Y (contracted by public sector)
Veterinary research	Public because of market failure (poverty focused)	Private for commercial purposes	Y	Y (contracted by public sector)

Source: Umali, Feder, and de Haan 1994.
Note: Y = Yes, acceptable; YY = Yes, strongly recommended.

Table 4.2 Impacts of Public Investments in Agriculture: China and India

	Economic benefit-cost ratio		Number leaving poverty per unit of expenditure[a]	
	China	India	China	India
R&D	9.59	13.45	6.79	84.5
Irrigation	1.88	1.36	1.33	9.7
Roads	8.83	5.31	3.22	123.8
Education	8.68	1.39	8.80	41.0
Electricity	1.26	0.26	2.27	3.8
Poverty loan	—	1.09	1.13	17.8

Source: Fan, Zhang, and Zhang 2002.
Note: — = not available.
a. For China, the number of poor reduced is per 10,000 yuan expenditure; for India, the number of poor reduced is per million Rupee expenditure.

Public-Private Partnerships to Promote Private Investment and Market Development

Many "temporary" market failures in the agricultural sector may justify either one-time or time-limited public investments to catalyze sustained private investment. These types of investments are particularly important in agriculture. Experience from market liberalization in a wide number of settings during the 1990s has shown that the private sector did not fill the gap left when the public sector ceased to perform certain functions, especially in agriculture and in the least-developed countries (Dorward et al. 2004).

As described in chapter 3, the need to overcome coordination failures has increased as the need to participate in food supply chains has grown. Coordination failures occur when farmers or processors are working in an isolated or disconnected way, or when complementary investments are not made by others at different stages in the supply chain (Dorward and Kydd 2002). These situations are pervasive in many rural areas, particularly in the case of long-term investments or investments for highly specific purposes, such as facilities for processing a particular product (Joffe and Jones 2004). In such situations, joint public-private action can reduce poverty by supporting institutions that reduce transactions costs and risks of private investment in critical services for smallholder agriculture, especially the costs of financial, input, and output transactions. This kind of investment often includes public support for goods and services that fall outside the standard economic definition of public goods. Examples include support within a specific marketing chain to build sustainable commercial relationships; business development services; and specific mechanisms, such as insurance, to limit the risks facing private investors.

Such investments must aim to cover only transactions costs and not distort long-run prices. They should aim to build institutional solutions that the private sector can maintain without public support after the initial phase. As market volume increases and institutional arrangements are strengthened, transactions costs and risks fall, and the state should withdraw to a regulatory role. If the state persists in providing "transitional" support, its intervention can soon become expensive and distorting.

Figure 4.2 is an overview of potential public-private interventions that can be made over a limited period. Because these investments build the demand for, and supply of, support services, they will strengthen market systems and encourage private investment. The key dilemma is how to identify, target, and implement useful investments accurately, in partnership with a range of other actors and in ways that are nondistorting, support market development, and benefit the poor over the long term (Joffe and Jones 2004).

The scope for using time-limited public-private investments includes:

- *public sector procurement arrangements* to outsource the supply of public services, such as extension services or pest and disease control, in order to stimulate private markets for services (for example, World Bank support to advisory services in Peru);
- *strengthening smallholders' links to the market* by building networks and providing development grants that improve coordination along the marketing chain, as in Operation Flood, a highly successful dairy project in India (see box 3.10);
- *piloting innovative financial institutions,* such as weather insurance for crops or livestock and commodity risk management programs, sometimes in cooperation with the IFC, to reduce price risks for commodities that are important for smallholders;
- *providing vouchers* through public works programs to the poorest and most vulnerable farmers to purchase fertilizer, as is being piloted in Malawi with IFDC and World Bank support; and
- *providing matching grants* for on-farm investments to promote the introduction of new products, especially to reduce poverty in marginal areas, as in projects undertaken in Mexico, Nigeria, and Tanzania with World Bank support.

As indicated by figure 4.2, both demand and supply must be stimulated at the same time for limited-time public investments to foster lasting

Figure 4.2 Entry Points for Demand- and Supply-Side Stimulation

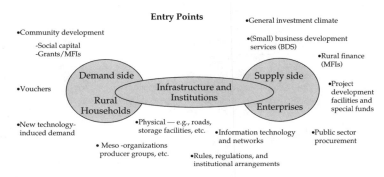

Source: Joffe and Jones 2004.

private investment and service provision (Joffe and Jones 2004). *Demand can be stimulated through*

- *linkage effects,* which induce demand through technical change or productivity growth near the beginning of the supply chain (e.g., in farmers' fields);
- *information and social capital,* which induce demand through a change in the perceived benefits and risks of a particular enterprise, perhaps through an agricultural extension campaign or institutional strengthening; and
- *subsidies* to induce demand through a temporary reduction in price or risks (e.g., through a grant or voucher program).

Enterprises will increase supply in response to any such increase in demand, depending on their capacity, level of entrepreneurship, availability of debt/equity financing, the investment climate, and public procurement policy.

Declining Allocations of Public Expenditures to Agriculture: Causes, Effects, and Solutions

As governments have reduced their intervention in agricultural markets, there has been a corresponding reduction in the share of public expenditure directed toward agriculture. In Asia and Latin America, the decline in public funding for agriculture partly reflects agriculture's declining importance in the

Table 4.3 Composition of Total Public Expenditures, 1980 and 1998 (percent)

	Africa 1980	Africa 1998	Asia 1980	Asia 1998	Latin America 1980	Latin America 1998
Agriculture	6	5	15	10	8	3
Education	12	16	14	20	16	19
Health	3	5	5	4	4	7
Transport and communications	6	4	12	5	11	6
Social Security	5	3	4	3	19	26
Defense	12	10	18	11	7	7
Other	55	57	33	47	35	32
	100	100	100	100	100	100
Agriculture						
—Ag value added (as % GDP)	17.6	18.8	33.2	19.5	10.4	7.9
—Ag spending (as % of ag GDP)	7.5	6.0	9.6	8.2	12.7	7.2

Source: Fan and Rao 2003.

economy. In Africa, agriculture's share in public spending fell even as its share in economic production rose, largely because farmers and consumers had only limited political clout and because more emphasis was placed on education, health, and social security (table 4.3 and discussion in chapter 6). Some countries, particularly China, have very recently increased the share of public funding for agriculture.

Declining public expenditures for agriculture are consistent with the structural transformation process, but the bias against expenditure for agriculture in Africa remains a major concern. Expenditures for agriculture began to fall in Africa long before countries had invested sufficiently in agricultural R&D and rural infrastructure for growth to occur (table 3.1), and expenditures have fallen despite much recent empirical evidence that the economic and social payoffs to agricultural investments are quite high (table 4.2). The recent agreement by the New Partnership for Africa's Development (NEPAD) to increase spending to 10 percent of national budgets is aimed at reversing this trend.

As welcome as initiatives to increase allocations to agriculture may be, the quality of public expenditures—in other words, the efficient use of available funds—is arguably even more important than the actual level of funding. Additional funding does not have a sustained and positive effect if, for example, investments crowd out private sector activities, are provided in an adverse business environment, or succumb to corruption and fraud (box 4.1). López (2004) estimates that about half of the public expenditures on agriculture in Latin America still consist of subsidies and private goods that benefit larger farmers. An increase of 1 percent in the share of public expenditures to agriculture in Latin America would raise the growth rate of agricultural production by 0.23 percent per capita, compared with the 0.06 percent increase from the current allocation (López 2004).

Public Investment in Physical Capital to Keep Agriculture Competitive

Poor physical infrastructure for transport, power, communications, irrigation, water, and sanitation severely constrains agricultural growth and poverty reduction in most low-income countries. The private sector and communities

---

Box 4.1 Making Public Expenditures on Agriculture More Effective in Zambia

About 70 percent of the Zambian population depends on agriculture, and Zambia is one of the few countries experiencing urban to rural migration. The country's combination of high-potential environments for agriculture and limited access to markets would seem to indicate that investments in improving market access would yield good returns. Yet agriculture's share of aggregate public expenditure has been only around 3 percent in recent years. Allocation of expenditures within the agricultural sector has been highly skewed toward ministry headquarters (which receive about two-thirds of the allocation), with agricultural extension, animal production and health, soils and crops research, and agricultural training each receiving about 5 percent. Disbursements are guided by the availability of funds and by subjective judgment, not by an established budget, thus reducing the credibility of the budgetary system.

A review of public expenditure recommended strict budgetary discipline, in which the budget is driven by activities and implemented according to plan. Public expenditure for agriculture would need to focus on removing the bottlenecks to agricultural development (e.g., transport costs) and removing such distortions in commercial markets as maize and fertilizer subsidies. Decreasing the fertilizer subsidy alone would free substantial resources for agricultural services and investments (e.g., in extension, research, feeder roads, and irrigation) that would support growth without displacing the private sector.

Source: World Bank internal documents.

Box 4.2 Rural Infrastructure: Key Areas for Investment

- *Irrigation water* is a major input to agricultural production. The availability of water is a political issue because water is strongly linked to food security, poverty reduction, and environmental conservation. Water is critical for maintaining a productive labor force and for processing agricultural products. Some marginal areas can develop or expand irrigation systems that will improve productivity and reduce vulnerability to erratic weather, and more partnerships are being formed with the private sector to invest in irrigation infrastructure for these and other areas. Such investments should extend beyond simply providing irrigation water to include provisions for managing the externalities associated with irrigated agriculture, such as drainage.

  Investment decisions should be made by the community or local government. Operations and maintenance should also be financed at the local level through user tariffs. Investments are needed to build capacity for agricultural water management. These range from supporting local water user associations (WUAs) to creating broad regulatory frameworks for the development of water markets.
- *Transportation,* especially road construction and improvement, reduces the time and expense of transporting products to the market and importing the necessary inputs. Better transportation systems facilitate labor migration and expand opportunities for off-farm employment.

  Ownership of these investments should rest with local governments or communities, though central agencies may help develop the overall strategy, provide financing, and offer technical support to increase the impact of transportation investments on reducing poverty. Maintenance should be financed at the local level, where levies, tolls, and other user fees may be appropriate to recover costs.
- *Power,* including electrification, is a critical input to irrigation. It also improves rural welfare in many other ways, and opens opportunities for producing new crops and processing agricultural products.

  More public-private financing strategies should be used to develop electricity grids, with the private sector taking a greater role in developing smaller "mini-grids" and solar power sources. Operating costs should be funded through tariffs.
- *Information and communication systems,* including postal and telecommunication services with mobile and Internet connectivity, make it easier to transmit information about prices, share information

(box continued next page)

(box continued)

about markets and how they are functioning, and coordinate input sourcing, labor management, and product marketing.

Investments and services should be provided by the private sector, with limited scope for community involvement. Funding should generally be through a user-pays system, though targeted subsidies may be appropriate to extend service to needy areas.

- *Processing infrastructure,* including systems for sorting, processing, packaging, storing, and certifying agricultural products, is needed to expand alternatives for rural livelihoods off of the farm.

Generally the private sector will be responsible for investment and operations. The role of central and local government will be to provide a policy environment conducive to investment. Producer and trade associations and groups can play an important role in determining what kind of infrastructure is most appropriate.

- *Social infrastructure,* such as health and education services, is essential for the well-being and productivity of the labor force and for building basic skills and knowledge.

Investment and operating responsibilities will vary according to the service provided. Central and local governments will need to cover the initial and recurrent costs, and in many cases full or partial subsidies will be important for providing some services.

Source: Authors; Fishbein 2001.

---

themselves can provide the bulk of resources for developing certain types of infrastructure (e.g., telecommunications, community infrastructure). Public investment in many of these goods is warranted, however, because they are generally useful to all members of society and not simply to the immediate beneficiaries, and because they help markets and the wider economy to function more efficiently. The lessons learned from investments in specific kinds of infrastructure, along with important issues in implementing investments, are summarized in box 4.2.

Irrigation is one of the major investments for keeping agriculture competitive while reducing poverty and sustaining natural resources. Irrigation investments encompass such diverse activities as expanding infrastructure, especially drainage; making institutional reforms that enhance the efficiency and equity of irrigation systems (e.g., strengthening WUAs); and developing technological innovations.[1] Although the scope for investing in irrigated farming systems is large, governments have reduced support for badly needed investments in irrigation and drainage in recent years (World Bank 2005a). An emerging alternative is to consider public-private partnerships such as the one formed by the government of Morocco and Omnium Nord-Africain (ONA), a Moroccan industrial conglomerate, to construct and manage a 10,000-hectare irrigation project (IFC 2004).

Aside from irrigation, investments in other types of rural infrastructure help reduce poverty through: (1) direct, daily effects on the welfare and livelihoods of the poor (e.g., safe drinking water); (2) support for developing social networks (e.g., communications); and (3) stimulation of agricultural intensification and diversification by lowering production and marketing costs (e.g., feeder roads).

Numerous studies have empirically illustrated the high returns to investments in rural infrastructure. Fan, Hazell, and Thorat (1999) showed that there were high returns (both economic payoffs and reduction in poverty) to investing in rural roads in India, particularly in less-favored areas. A study on the returns to infrastructure investments in China (Fan, Zhang, and Zhang 2002) showed that, after education, investment in rural infrastructure (roads, electricity, and telecommunications) had the largest impact on reducing rural poverty. Given that many countries have limited capacity and resources to make immediate investments in infrastructure, it will take many decades of massive investment to overcome infrastructure constraints, especially in Africa. Complementary institutions and technologies are urgently needed to mitigate the limitations currently imposed by inadequate infrastructure (box 4.3).

Previous attempts to develop infrastructure have been mixed. Many failures occurred in operation and maintenance. Approaches have now moved away from large-scale, ultimately unsustainable operations to smaller, more focused investments that are developed with the intended beneficiaries and include measures to sustain operation and maintenance. *Experience with investing in physical infrastructure has identified three prerequisites for enhancing the sustainability and equitability of these investments: decentralization, participation, and targeting the poor.*

- *Decentralization:* Because the needs for rural infrastructure are typically too dispersed and small to be met through central planning, implementation, and management, it is important to decentralize these functions. The political, fiscal, and administrative aspects of decentralization will vary according to the nature and objectives of the investment (box 4.4), but decentralization must be framed within a clear and consistent rural infrastructure strategy that strikes a balance between tailoring infrastructure projects to local needs and ensuring

Box 4.3 Massive Investments Are Needed for Africa's Rural Infrastructure to Reach Levels of India over 50 Years Ago

The lack of energy, transport, water, sanitation, and telecommunications services remains especially limiting in Africa, even in comparison with access to these services in the years immediately after independence in India (see inset table). Only a massive program of investment over many decades, especially for rural roads and irrigation systems, can close this gap. In the meantime, it is particularly urgent to develop technologies that help rural people use inputs and infrastructure more efficiently.

Africa: Road Density and Access to Water and Sanitation

	Improved sanitation facilities, rural[a]	Improved water source, rural[a]	Road density (km/1000 sq. km)	Road density required to match that of India in 1950
	2000	2000	Early 1990s	
Benin	6	55	36	291
Cameroon	66	39	38	168
Côte d'Ivoire	35	72	94	258
Ghana	70	62	17	429
Mozambique	26	41	17	135
Nigeria	45	49	97	718
Sierra Leone	53	46	80	391
Tanzania	86	57	66	181
Zambia	64	48	36	110
Madagascar	30	31	67	137

Source: Spencer 1994; World Bank 2003a.
a. Percentage of rural population with access.

that they can be scaled up for wider coverage. Investments in rural infrastructure often fail because decision making has been decentralized but local authorities cannot command adequate revenues to maintain infrastructure. For this reason, rural infrastructure strategies must also determine the appropriate sequence of investments and synergies among them (for example, irrigation schemes for perishable

---

Box 4.4 Tanzania: Decentralization Puts Roads on the Map Again

Since 1998, Tanzania has rehabilitated up to 530 miles of rural roads in 23 districts and constructed 107 bridges under a USAID program. Transportation costs in the target areas have been reduced by about 40 percent on average. More importantly, the program has successfully involved local district governments and the private sector in managing road maintenance and rehabilitation. Today the private sector is involved in more than 80 percent of the district road rehabilitation and maintenance that occurs under this program. One reason for this success is that the project helped to build capacity in local districts to prepare, tender, and award bids and to supervise road rehabilitation and maintenance contracts. Recent consultations have found that academics, policy makers, and development practitioners in Tanzania applaud the program.

Source: IFPRI 2002.

---

products can be developed in sequence with improved roads to get the produce to the market).

- *Participation, commitment, and accountability:* Local participation in the design, financing, implementation, and management of infrastructure are critical to success. In northeast Brazil, the pillars of a sustainable infrastructure project that also sought to reduce poverty were demand-driven decisions, gender inclusiveness, and assurances of payment (including payment of maintenance costs) (box 4.5). As in the case of Brazil, strengthening user associations (particularly for irrigation) often is an important step toward improving local participation and ensuring that service providers are accountable.

- *Targeting the poor:* In low-income countries with widespread poverty, broad investments in rural infrastructure are likely to make substantial inroads on poverty, and special targeting might not be needed. In a country such as Madagascar, where 90 percent of the rural population lives under the poverty line, any investment in rural infrastructure would have a major impact on poverty (table 4.4). In countries experiencing increasing regional differentiation, however, infrastructure projects might be advised to concentrate on poorer regions, use local labor as much as possible, include differential pricing for the poor in cost recovery schemes, and ensure that the poor have a strong voice in decision making. Focusing investment on the poor will reduce the feasibility

Box 4.5 Brazil: Empowering Communities to Reach Their Development Objectives

The Rural Poverty Alleviation Program in northeast Brazil supports rural and agricultural development objectives through decentralization, matching grants, participation, and ownership. This program, an early champion of community-driven development (CDD), started in 1985 as a small pilot component of the Northeast Rural Development Program (NRDP). The pilot project transferred resources directly to community associations. Activities were financed through a Fund for Community Support that operated along three lines: mobilization and organization of producers and communities; productive subprojects, including agricultural production, agro-processing and handicrafts; and investments (mainly in infrastructure) that would be useful for the larger community.

The pilot project became the template for radically redesigning the NRDP. The redesigned program covered all members of poor rural communities, not just individuals with productive assets, by linking matching grants to beneficiaries' contributions toward the costs of subprojects. The matching grants were provided directly to community associations to finance small subprojects identified by the association in a participatory manner.

The socioeconomic benefits of the Rural Poverty Alleviation Program have been significant. More than 44,000 subprojects (77 percent infrastructure, 20 percent productive, and 3 percent social) were completed, benefiting about 7.5 million people over the long term in a sustainable way. These investments generated some 100,000 additional permanent jobs and increased cultivated area by more than 80,000 hectares. Moreover, these investments generated additional, sustainable, annual income or savings of more than US$200 million. Typical small subprojects to provide tractors and irrigation have yielded annual net income or savings exceeding US$20,000. Another impressive aspect of the program is its low overhead cost (7 percent of total funds), meaning that 93 percent of available funds goes directly to the communities. A less tangible but no less important achievement has been the establishment of a decentralized approach to resource allocation. Municipal governments are now more accustomed to participatory decision making in which community associations increasingly voice their needs.

Source: World Bank 2004b.

of recovering costs directly, however. It will be necessary to consider the tradeoffs between implementing infrastructure projects to reduce poverty and implementing projects that can be sustained in the absence of continued donor or public sector funding.

Table 4.4 Effect of Remoteness on Farming Systems and Poverty in Madagascar

Remoteness	Travel time to nearest city (hrs)	Transport cost as % rice price	Household subsistence ratio	Number of livestock per household	Percent poor
1 Least remote	1	2	20	1.2	54
2	3	15	37	2.3	77
3	9	16	38	2.9	85
4	16	19	41	6.1	85
5 Most remote	32	28	42	5.6	86

Source: Stifel, Minten, and Dorosh 2003.

Public Investment in Human and Social Capital to Benefit the Poor

The human and social capital needed for growth that benefits the poor includes the health and education of the workforce, the talent of local entrepreneurs, the capacity of civil servants, the competence of leaders in local associations, and the availability of information for sound policy and investment decisions. Investment in these "soft" assets generally provides high returns, but it involves complex processes with costs that are spread over many years.

Investment in Health Keeps Agriculture Working

Because agriculture in developing countries depends so highly on labor, healthy agricultural workers are essential if labor productivity is to improve and people are to move out of poverty.

Improvements in delivering health care to rural areas requires the participation of women, who usually provide health and prevention services at the household level and are typically responsible for household nutrition. Investments in women's health, especially in reproductive health and the prevention of HIV/AIDS, are an important component of agricultural productivity. Agricultural extension programs must not only educate the rural population about HIV/AIDS prevention. They must also develop and disseminate agricultural practices that are adapted to the available supply of labor, with particular attention to the labor capacity of orphans and widows in areas ravaged by the disease. Several donor-supported projects in Africa have developed such programs.

Changes in agricultural practices can also be important in enhancing food security and nutrition, which are critical to the health of agricultural households. For example, micronutrient deficiencies can be overcome through greater emphasis on producing fruits and vegetables and through the development of varieties with higher nutrient content. In eastern Africa, the spread of sweet potato varieties rich in beta-carotene, especially among women farmers, has helped overcome vitamin A deficiencies (Hagenimana et al. 1999). Finally, the introduction of sustainable agricultural practices, especially with respect to pesticides, reduces rural households' exposure to health risks.

Investment in Education Keeps Agriculture Competitive

A second critical element for improving labor productivity is education and training for agriculturalists. Numerous studies have shown high returns to improving farmers' information and skills so that they can use technologies more efficiently. In settings where agriculture is changing rapidly and becoming increasingly knowledge-intensive, additional education for men and women generally has a strong and significant effect on technical knowledge, technology adoption, and farm productivity (Hussain and Byerlee 1995). A wide range of approaches to providing skills and education (formal and informal, primary and secondary) can provide high payoffs to public investments.

The content of agricultural education will have to shift markedly, however. Farmers, agribusiness entrepreneurs, and farm laborers must learn how to meet changing market demand rather than to simply increase current production. If they do not, producers will be ill prepared to substitute such knowledge-intensive practices as integrated pest management for less appropriate and less productive practices, such as increased pesticide use. Investments in higher education are also needed if the agricultural population is to determine whether to take advantage of the novel technologies that rapid advances in science, such as genomics, promise to deliver. New competencies are also needed in business planning and management, networking and communications, and sectoral economics and policies.

Despite the clear need and potential for investing in human capital to meet these goals, numerous hurdles remain. In many countries, the activities of agencies involved in agricultural education (ministries of agriculture and of education) are poorly coordinated and rarely integrated with activities of R&D agencies. Goals for improving education and training systems are rarely incorporated into national strategies to develop the agricultural sector, leading to uncoordinated investments in three fundamental and interlinked agricultural areas: research, extension, and higher education. A piecemeal approach to institution building has often created poorly sequenced, dysfunctional, oversized, and generally unsustainable agricultural institutions in Africa (Eicher 2004).

Although agricultural education has such a critical role to play, the World Bank's lending in agricultural education and training over 1995–2004 was US$82 million for education, compared with about US$2.9 billion for research and extension. This disparity arose partly because the Bank's organizational structure presents challenges for accommodating cross-sectoral investments such as those needed to improve agricultural education. *The critical lesson for the future is that the Bank must develop internal collaboration between its rural and human development staff, and it must partner with and re-engage other organizations to support coordinated approaches to agricultural education and capacity building.*

Investment in Civil Service Capacity Keeps Agriculture on Track

A chronic and, in some areas, worsening constraint on agricultural stakeholders' participation in setting national policies and investment priorities is the lack of qualified people. Often civil servants with the appropriate skills are not available to formulate national and sectoral policies, guide the development of institutions, and design quality investments that can deliver growth and benefit the poor.

To support agriculture more successfully, civil servants must expand and reorient their skills, sometimes in conjunction with downsizing in agricultural agencies. With the changing role of the state, civil servants for agriculture require a wider repertoire of skills, including skills in forging partnerships with the private sector, in negotiating international and bilateral agreements, in defining the public good element in public expenditures, and in facilitating participatory development of a strategy for agriculture with wide support from stakeholders. *Experience shows that efforts to build capacity for public sector decision making in agriculture tend to be more successful when they:*

- use demand-driven and participatory approaches to identify gaps in skills of civil servants and to build relevant capacities;
- pay particular attention to improving the skills in negotiation, communication, and organization that will ease collaboration among ministries (such as ministries of agriculture, trade, and natural resources) and represent these sectors more effectively in global and regional negotiations;
- coordinate donors' efforts to develop consistent and continuous programs for building capacity, avoiding "unfair" competition from long-term technical assistance;

- provide effective incentives with respect to salaries, performance incentives, hiring and firing practices, and the introduction of transparent accountability processes in the public service; and
- include mechanisms to allow the public sector to contract out some functions (like policy research) to capable, local entities, including consulting firms, NGOs, and universities.

Investment in Social Capital Strengthens Agricultural Stakeholders

The roles of social capital[2] and stakeholder organizations (which can include community-based organizations, rural producer organizations, WUAs, business partnerships, and trade associations) are particularly important in agriculture because of the sheer number of individual households involved in agricultural activities. Effective social organization makes it easier for people to cooperate and coordinate their activities for mutual benefit, and it often enhances the benefits of investments in other forms of capital. As mentioned in chapter 3, collective action helps the poor participate in markets from which they would otherwise be excluded. CDD funds often are effective in catalyzing the formation of meaningful local organizations from the ground up, rather than imposing them artificially from above. CDD funds are available to communities, usually in the form of matching grants, to implement subprojects of their choosing (see below). Support to producer and community groups should pay attention to common causes of failure, such as the lack of inclusiveness or the propensity for powerful local interests to capture the benefits, and an exit strategy will be essential for avoiding continued subsidies and dependency.

Public Investment in Natural Capital to Sustain the Environment

As the natural resources used in agriculture are often public or common pool goods that can be used by any and all people, much of the investment in sustaining or improving natural resources should be cofinanced by the public sector. At the farm level, rural households will invest in improving natural resources if it is profitable, although the technologies and approaches that they use are often based on those developed by the public sector (box 4.6). These include conservation tillage, integrated pest and disease management, and innovations in irrigation to improve water use efficiency.

At the more general level, public investments in watershed management, agroforestry, payment systems for environmental services, and

---

Box 4.6 Ways to Invest in Natural Capital at the Farm Level

Integrated pest management (IPM) considers multiple aspects of the ecosystem in managing pest and disease problems, and it emphasizes monitoring before resorting to biological or chemical means of control. The combination of techniques used in IPM includes monitoring pest populations against economic thresholds; modifying cultural practices; and using resistant varieties, habitat manipulation, and biological control. Less toxic chemical pesticides are used only when monitoring indicates that they are needed. Implementation issues concern the high transactions costs, as this technology is highly specific to each individual site and highly knowledge intensive. The farmer-to-farmer transmission of IPM knowledge has also been found to be less effective than expected (Feder, Murgai, and Quizon 2004).

Conservation farming encompasses four broad, intertwined management practices: minimal soil disturbance (no plowing and harrowing), maintaining a permanent vegetative soil cover, direct sowing, and sound crop rotation. This technology is now widely adopted in some parts of the developing world, such as Brazil.

Low external input and sustainable agriculture (LEISA) uses farmers' knowledge and a range of management practices (agroforestry, IPM, intercropping, crop-livestock integration, microclimate management) to minimize the need for purchased inputs.

Organic agriculture employs agronomic, biological, and mechanical methods in crop and livestock production to control pests and maintain soil fertility without using any synthetic chemicals.

Source: Authors.

---

rangeland and livestock development for pastoralists all entail investments in natural capital. For instance, integrated watershed management has been successfully supported by the World Bank in India, Latin America, North Africa, and West Asia. It encompasses a range of practices, combining water harvesting, groundwater recharge, and the use of vegetative cover with the development of viable agricultural systems to increase agricultural carrying capacity, although the long-term sustainability of these activities is still somewhat uncertain. With this caveat, conservation farming and watershed development are now ready for scaling up to other areas.

These agricultural investments, probably more than any others, require decentralized approaches for planning and service delivery. Most natural resource

---

Box 4.7 Turkey: Restoring Watersheds and Forests in Eastern Anatolia

In 1993, Turkey launched the Eastern Anatolia Watershed Rehabilitation Project with World Bank support to help restore sustainable range, forest, and farming activities in the upper watersheds of three provinces. These goals would be achieved by reducing soil degradation, erosion, and sedimentation in reservoirs, and by increasing productivity and incomes in this impoverished region of Turkey. Using a participatory approach, the project was designed to strengthen farmers' capacity for planning and implementation while improving the responsiveness of rural service agencies to farmers' needs.

The project established community participation processes that involved consultation, and it also encouraged villages in microwatershed catchments to use problem-solving techniques for interaction. The project succeeded strongly in introducing a participatory approach in a very traditional society and in achieving exceptional institutional coordination. It supported the planting of nearly 100,000 hectares of trees and the use of other conservation practices on forest department land, exceeding the target by about 50 percent. It also provided substantial funding for activities that supported agriculture, including irrigation, partly to compensate rural people for the loss of benefits from closed forested areas. These achievements should reduce soil loss and flooding. The largest impact is likely to occur in the longer term and cannot yet be measured. The project's main weaknesses, which provide important lessons for future projects, include failure to achieve any significant portion of the substantial planned rangeland rehabilitation, partly because land tenure issues could not be resolved; limited progress on including women and poorer households; and concerns about the sustainability of the project at the *community and government level*.

Source: World Bank internal document.

---

management problems are site-specific, requiring collective decisions by users and a high level of managerial input and adaptation to local ecological, economic, and social circumstances.[3] The World Bank–funded Eastern Anatolia Watershed Rehabilitation Project in Turkey (box 4.7), which featured participatory watershed management planning, succeeded in introducing new land management technologies and also provided a framework to monitor performance against specific indicators. Local government institutions decided how they could most effectively deliver natural resource management services based on the stated needs of the community.

Matching Grants to Provide Public
Goods and Income

Over the past decade, mechanisms for financing public goods have under-
gone a distinct shift. Annual budget appropriations and donor support for
specific projects to be implemented by public organizations and ministries
have been supplanted by the use of competitive grants that engage the
public and private sector in implementation. Grants are also being used as
time-limited support for overcoming temporary market failures and catalyzing sustained private sector investment. Nearly half of the World
Bank's lending for agriculture includes grants of one form or another.

*Grants offer opportunities for using public funds to finance the provision of
public goods by the private sector or to match private investments until efficient
financial and risk markets emerge.* To make economic sense, grant schemes
have to generate social benefits over and above those that private
providers alone would have been willing to generate (Phillips 2001). For
example, the use of grants to support micro- and small enterprises is often
justified to redress problems arising from limited economies of scale, lack
of market power, lack of information, and poverty reduction. However,
grant schemes generally tread a thin line between "tipping the balance"
toward enterprises with clear commercial potential and wasting public
funds on projects that private banks could accommodate, or, even worse,
crowding out the private banking sector.

In the agricultural sector, grants have been used for three main
purposes: agricultural innovation (i.e., technology development), business and market development, and community-driven investment in
income-generating activities or in local infrastructure (van der Meer and
Noordam 2004). To meet these three objectives, grants may help to facilitate training, access to technology and information, innovation, project
preparation, participation in trade fairs, investment in local infrastructure, investment in networks, and collective action for mutual benefits
with spillover effects. Box 4.8 presents guidelines for the use of matching
grants.

Grants for private goods currently used in production processes (e.g.,
construction materials, fuel, and fertilizers) generally are not justified,
though in some cases small grants are directed to the poorest to enhance
their access to productive assets or to pilot test innovations.

Matching grant systems are likely to work best when the general business environment is relatively supportive and initiatives of this kind are
targeted to particular groups. The government needs a relatively sophis-
ticated capacity to develop a strategic vision to guide and coordinate
grant initiatives, as well as the capacity to design, monitor, evaluate, and
manage them. Grant-based approaches should thus not be seen as

---

Box 4.8 Steps to Create Successful Grant Programs

- The type of grant selected should be tailored to local circumstances, including the quality of local technical expertise.
- The economic rationale for public co-financing should be articulated clearly within the public sector.
- Rigorous and transparent eligibility criteria and assessment procedures are very important, as is competent fund management with clear objectives and procedures.
- To ensure that proposals address private sector priorities, an initial investment may be desirable to build the capacity of potential recipients so that they can develop and defend proposals that identify and define problems, critically evaluate alternative solutions, and justify grant funding based on clear net benefits in economic and social terms.
- A significant learning period should be allowed to enable stakeholders to gain experience in working with the grant scheme and to make adjustments to the way grants are managed as necessary.
- Administrative costs must be controlled rigorously to create a sustainable private market for support services within a limited period. Fifteen percent appears to be an international norm for start-up and staffing costs, administering grants, monitoring and evaluation, institutional development, and training to prepare proposals.
- Often there are tradeoffs between ensuring that operations are cost-effective and ensuring that they are conducted with accountability and transparency. Some balance must be sought to ensure that both objectives are met.
- Grant funding is typically most effective when it is complemented by other funding mechanisms. In many cases, block funding from the public sector will still be needed to address core market failures and policy objectives.
- From the beginning, grant schemes should have a clear disengagement strategy. Proposals should include action steps that can be monitored, with milestones and targets indicating when objectives have been achieved.

Sources: Authors; McKean and Ostrom 1995; van der Meer and Noordam 2004.

---

replacements for a wider process of capacity building and institutional strengthening (Joffe and Jones 2004).

Grants for Agricultural Innovation

Competitive grants for research and extension have been used extensively in donor-funded projects in recent years to tap underused capacity and skills in public and private organizations, as well as to increase the quality

---

Box 4.9 Ecuador: Competitive Grants

The Program for Modernization of Agricultural Services in Ecuador finances a competitive research grants program that has funded 112 research projects. The program has supported strategic work on innovations to open new export markets by controlling the fruit fly (which affects cherimoya, guava, zapote, and other Andean fruits), decreasing production costs for new export products (snails, tree tomatoes, babaco, mushrooms, and artichokes), and controlling diseases and insects in traditional export crops (banana, cacao, and coffee).

The program introduced a new research culture and brought new organizations into the research system. Research projects are executed by 45 public and private organizations, with most projects directly linked to potential users of the technologies. The government contracted with a private agency to manage the program, develop procedures, and monitor implementation. This role was eventually taken over by the Ministry of Agriculture. Research project costs averaged US$116,000, of which 54 percent is financed by grants and 46 percent by executing agencies, mostly through in-kind contributions. By leveraging cofinancing for research projects, the program has helped to increase national research funding by 92 percent to approximately 0.54 percent of agricultural GDP.

Source: World Bank internal documents.

---

and relevance of agricultural research. Many of these grants have been channeled either directly to farmers' associations, or through partnerships with them, to ensure that local demand increasingly guides the development and dissemination of technology. This approach has met with considerable success, especially in funding research. To be sustained, it requires local public and private financial support and a highly professional unit to administer the program (box 4.9).

Grants for Business Development Services

Unlike providing grants to spur agricultural innovation, providing government or donor grants to develop agribusiness has produced mixed results. Such grants can impede the development of a sustainable market for support services and fail to improve the capabilities of recipient firms in a significant way. Government and donor perceptions, rather than the demand expressed by enterprises, tend to determine the kinds of services that are provided (box 4.10). These problems are being addressed through the use of vouchers and special "user funds." Providing vouchers to

---

**Box 4.10 Chile: Matching Grants for Small-
and Medium-Size Enterprises (SMEs)**

The matching grant scheme in Chile was executed at first by a public
agency. Following a series of implementation problems (lack of cost sharing, lack of client input in selecting consultants, and virtually no market
orientation), its execution was gradually outsourced to private entities.
The government retained discretionary decision-making power, however,
which reduced the executing agents' autonomy and diluted the program's
transparency. The scheme was designed to support a broad range of advisory services, focusing primarily on SMEs. The executing agents were
given an administration fee of 15 percent of the overall project costs—a
dramatic cost reduction from the previous state-run scheme.

Source: World Bank internal documents.

---

potential users of business services can improve the demand for services
as well as the quality of service rendered. Vouchers can also be used to
support market development and training, thus encouraging constructive
competition between service and training providers. Special user funds
enable producer organizations to propose market development services
and capacity-building activities (e.g., study tours, training programs)
with co-financing from farmers. These funds enable the group to contract
with service providers (often NGOs) and make them more accountable.

Grants for Community-Driven Development

Experience with implementing CDD programs indicates that funds are
best allocated to communities by the public sector based on a broad set of
clear and transparent criteria, either using a negative list of items that cannot be financed or a broad positive list.

The use of CDD-type grants has been particularly strong in rural areas
and therefore in agriculture. In rural areas, the distance from central agencies makes grassroots planning and implementation even more relevant
than in urban areas. Communities typically have expressed demand for
small-scale social and economic infrastructure, but they increasingly identify income-generating activities as priorities. Although direct transfers
for productive activities may be justified if they reduce poverty by targeting the very poor, and although they can generate some private sector
development, it is important to recognize that much care should be taken

to prevent them from undermining a culture of financial discipline, increasing dependency, and crowding out the development of sustainable microfinance institutions.

By encouraging collective action (e.g., producer organizations) for technical support, the purchase of inputs, and marketing, CDD grants can provide options that are not open to individuals acting alone. Experience so far indicates a reasonably good record with groups undertaking commercial activities, as in the CDD programs in northeast Brazil (box 4.5), but there has been much less success with groups focusing on community-managed natural resources. In any case, related investments in capacity building are often needed to complement the CDD approach and prepare communities and local government for participatory appraisal and implementation. Complementary funding may also be required for infrastructure beyond the community level.

Entry Points for Public Policy

Evidence is mounting that investments in core public goods—in infrastructure, education, and natural resources—have high payoffs in the form of economic growth and reduced poverty. Yet most countries, especially in Africa, still underinvest in public goods for agriculture. A larger share of public expenditures must be allocated to the agricultural sector, especially in Africa, and current resources must be managed more effectively by shifting resources from private goods and subsidies to public goods.

A more balanced approach to agricultural investments is based on a greatly improved understanding of the distribution of responsibilities between public and private enterprises and civil society. Effective public investments also require institutional developments such as decentralization, participation, and public-private partnerships. A variety of new public-private partnerships is allowing the public sector to leverage private investments and strengthen the market orientation of its investments. Time-limited matching grants to the private sector and to communities are becoming a particularly popular way for donors to support agricultural development.

The lessons learned from these efforts are that considerable care must be taken to ensure that grants support market development, are administered transparently and efficiently, are not captured by elites, and provide satisfactory economic returns. New tools and criteria are needed for improving the design and evaluation of grant schemes to ensure that they are compatible with market principles. Finally, a much greater effort is required to evaluate these experiences rigorously and learn how to improve the design of future investments (Mansuri and Rao 2004).

Key tasks for the future are to bring current good practices into a much broader national, regional, or international framework, and to move donor funding toward direct budgetary support and away from specific, well-controlled investments. The many examples in this chapter, and the wide-ranging investment options described in the *Agricultural Investment Sourcebook* (World Bank 2004b), demonstrate that a good body of experience is available to guide and scale up investments in physical, human, natural, and social capital. Even so, additional evaluation will be useful to refine and expand approaches for working with the private sector, to further develop financial systems for smallholder agriculture and agribusiness, and to establish criteria for matching grant systems that benefit the poor without leading to distortions in the wider economy. Finally, as agriculture becomes a far more knowledge-intensive enterprise, agricultural education will become much more critical to its success. Much greater coordination and integration is needed across sectors and agencies at the national and donor level to devise meaningful investments in agricultural education.

Getting Policies, Institutions, and Investments Right

In realizing agriculture's potential to foster economic growth that benefits the poor, the most formidable challenge is to maximize synergies among policies, institutions, and investments. Chapters 3 and 4 have emphasized that a major concern is to determine the most effective sequence for implementing and packaging policy reforms, institutional development, and public investments to fit local contexts. Setting the right policies while failing to develop and empower institutions will spur economic growth that favors advantaged groups and fails to advance marginalized groups. Empowerment without sound policy and public investment will merely empower the poor to control their present meager resources. In an unstable policy environment, investments are unlikely to yield sustainable returns.

The international development community can support comprehensive programs to assess which policy reforms, institutional improvements, and supporting investments are required in particular circumstances. For example, support for country-owned national agricultural strategies is a key entry point for the World Bank and other donors, discussed in chapters 3 and 6. The participatory development of national agricultural strategies is fundamental for capturing the unique circumstances, priorities, and investment requirements for each country (or state or district) and for effectively sequencing and packaging reforms and investments. The next chapter will discuss these sequencing and packaging issues in greater detail for different agricultural contexts.

5
Tailoring Development Support to Diverse Agricultural Systems

In this chapter

Three megasystems—irrigated high-potential agriculture, medium- to high-potential areas with limited market access, and marginal drylands—together account for over 3.3 billion people (73 percent of the population in agriculture in developing and transitional economies) and about 6 billion hectares. Priorities for each system include:

- *In irrigated high-potential areas,* which have good infrastructure, the most important strategy is to diversify on and off of the farm. On the farm, higher-value products can be produced. Off of the farm, diversification presents new opportunities for adding value and creating employment in rural areas. Growth in high-potential areas is driven basically by the private sector, so the priority for public policy is to eliminate remaining trade and market policy constraints and to invest in public goods that encourage private investments. The greatest policy challenge is to include the poor, especially in expanding markets for higher value commodities.
- *Medium- to high-potential areas with limited market access,* especially in Africa, represent a major priority and challenge for the development community. The two primary strategies—intensification and diversification—are aided by better access to input and output markets, complemented by the development of effective systems to generate and disseminate technologies. Aside from investing in infrastructure and technology, the main entry points should be supporting options for managing risk, developing land markets, and improving land management to mitigate land degradation. It is critically important to sequence these interventions carefully, especially to get markets working.
- *Marginal drylands,* where some of the world's poorest people live, present especially difficult challenges. Exit from agriculture is by far the most important strategy, followed by growth in off-farm employment. As exiting agriculture is generally a longer-term proposition, those

(box continued next page)

(box continued)

agricultural systems that remain viable must be developed in the short
and medium term to reduce poverty. The main hurdle for marginal
areas (and their often minority populations) is to involve them in the
policy dialogue and to design safety nets that do not encourage
dependency or crowd out local private initiatives.

Agricultural production contexts are distinguished by a host of variables,
but natural and human resource endowments, access to input and output
markets, and the use of technologies are among the primary ones.[1] Based
on these variables, three very broad types of agricultural systems can be
delineated: high-potential irrigated systems, high- and medium-potential
systems with limited access to markets, and marginal drylands. This
chapter describes these megasystems and discusses pathways for encouraging economic growth and reducing poverty in each one.

The discussion recognizes the difficulties of identifying integrated
approaches for systems that in reality are not as uniform as depicted here,
and that often exist in varying combinations in a given country. There is
clearly a need to analyze, prioritize, and sequence alternative investment
and policy options for specific contexts. For this reason, this chapter iden-
tifies and prioritizes the few elements that are most critical to overcoming
key bottlenecks and constraints limiting development in each type of system. The objective is to provide useful suggestions for decision makers
and others who must determine the specific practical steps needed for
agriculture to contribute to economic and social development in a given
region or country.

Three Agricultural Megasystems

From smallholder farming or pastoralism in marginal environments to
agricultural enterprises producing higher-quality, perishable goods for
export, the large variety of farming systems presents widely differing
challenges, opportunities, and entry points. *Building on a 2001 study by
FAO and the World Bank (Dixon, Gibbon, and Gulliver 2001), three agricultural
megasystems were selected based on resource potential and degree of market
access (table 5.1): irrigated high-potential systems, high-and medium-potential
systems with limited access to markets, and marginal drylands.*[2]

Agriculture in most countries will encompass some combination of these
systems,[3] which together account for over 3.3 billion people (73 percent

Table 5.1 Characteristics of Agriculture in Three Megasystems

Megasystem	Total area (million hectares)	Cultivated area (% total hectares)	Irrigated area as percentage of total cultivated area (%)	Total population (million)	Population per square kilometer	Agricultural population (million)	Agricultural population per cultivated hectares	Agricultural population (% total)
Irrigated high-potential	653	31	62	2,058	315	1,063	5.2	
High-and medium-potential, low market access	2,456	12	8	928	38	567	1.9	61
Marginal drylands	2,835	4	14	395	14	196	1.8	50
Other systems	3,972	13	13	1,628	41	667	1.3	41
TOTAL	**9,916**	**11**	**21**	**5,009**	**51**	**2,493**	**2.2**	**50**

Source: Computed from data provided by FAO based on Dixon, Gibbon, and Gulliver 2001.

of the population in agriculture in developing and transitional economies) and about 6 billion hectares (table 5.1). Other systems are by no means unimportant but are excluded from this analysis because of their diversity and relatively smaller size. Included in this "other" category are systems such as medium-potential areas with good market access, urban-based farming systems, and coastal artisanal fishing systems. Major farming systems that fall within each of the three megasystems are described in annex 1.

Another way of viewing strategic priorities is by market orientation. According to many in the development community, three "rural worlds" are emerging: commercial farmers and agribusiness; small-scale, market-oriented farmers who also produce for home consumption; and subsistence-oriented farmers whose first priority is to produce for home consumption with limited participation in the market (box 5.1). These "rural worlds" are found in each of the three megasystems discussed above. However, commercial farmers are more likely to be found in high-potential areas with good market access, whereas subsistence-oriented farmers are more commonly found in the more marginal areas. Across this spectrum of agricultural systems, the challenge for the development community is to provide an environment that helps the private sector serve commercial farmers and that concentrates public resources on serving the poor by (1) improving the incomes and reducing the vulnerability of small-scale, market-oriented farmers; and (2) enabling subsistence-oriented farmers to enter the market or exit agriculture altogether. *This report focuses on measures for empowering and helping small-scale farmers and subsistence-oriented farmers within the constraints of the three megasystems.*

Five Pathways to Foster Agricultural Growth in Different Contexts

Development pathways for agricultural systems will differ in terms of their relative importance and likely impact on poverty. Five pathways (Dixon, Gibbon, and Gulliver 2001) are discussed in this report:

- *Intensification* occurs when production from existing systems is increased. Kelley and Byerlee (2003) further differentiate between intensification that is driven by the generation of new technologies for existing enterprises, and intensification led by investments that relax key binding constraints, such as an investment in irrigation.
- *Diversification* is a change in resource use patterns and outputs that enables producers to take advantage of market opportunities.

Box 5.1 Farmers of "Three Rural Worlds"

Various models have been used to classify farming types, and they present different points of entry for helping the poor. Berdegue and Escobar (2001) categorize farm types according to their asset base and access to markets. *Commercial farmers* produce entirely for the market and prosper in a market-friendly environment, with good physical infrastructure, efficient financial institutions, and the protection of property rights. *Smallholder farm households* are linked to markets, but their farming practices are largely constrained by liquidity, risk, and transactions costs. These producers make joint production and consumption decisions, so household and farm activities are not easy to separate. Often subsistence food production is a response to the high transactions costs and risks of participating in markets. With improved market opportunities and greater support services, many of these farmers can build their asset base, adopt production processes that are more suitable to the environment, and make the transition to commercially oriented farming. *Subsistence-oriented farmers* frequently operate in less-favored and marginal production environments with poor access to markets. These households have unstable production and frequently suffer from food insecurity. The need to produce food for home consumption sometimes forces households to produce commodities that may not be suited to their natural resource base.

Source: Berdegue and Escobar 2001.

Diversification may or may not lead to specialization at the farm level, but throughout local regions it is likely to result in a greater diversity of enterprises because the quality of resources and access to them will vary within the region. The potential gains from diversification come from improving crop rotations, spreading labor demand, improving cash flows, and reducing risks.

- *Expansion of farm size* can occur when land is consolidated among a declining farm population or when farming expands into previously nonagricultural areas. Farm expansion is generally the least important strategy in irrigated and marginal systems, but it is still quite relevant in high-potential rainfed areas, such as those in Brazil and parts of Africa.
- *Off-farm income* can be obtained through seasonal migration as well as part-time employment in the local nonfarm economy. Typical income-earning activities include work in local agricultural processing plants, small-scale handicraft production, participation in the local service industry, remittances from migrants at distant locations, and employment in public works.

- *Exit* is the abandonment of farming for nonfarm occupations. Although exit can imply migration to a new location, usually a town or city, it can also simply mean the reallocation of labor to the rural non-farm economy within the local area.

The critical strategies and priorities for each megasystem are summarized in annex 2.

Agricultural Growth in Irrigated High-Potential Systems

Intensification in irrigated areas[4] has driven agricultural growth and catalyzed much wider macroeconomic growth and poverty reduction in many developing countries, especially in Asia.

Defining Characteristics of the System

Irrigated high-potential systems are estimated to cover 18 percent of cultivated land, but 43 percent of the total agricultural population in developing countries resides in these areas, mainly in Asia (figure 5.1). As one would expect, these areas are well endowed with natural resources. Their fertile soils and flat plains seem designed for high-yielding, intensive agriculture. Crops can often be grown year round (for up to three harvests per year). People generally have more equitable access to land and water than they do in other agricultural systems that face greater constraints.

Figure 5.1 High-Potential Irrigated Areas: Agricultural Population Distribution by Region

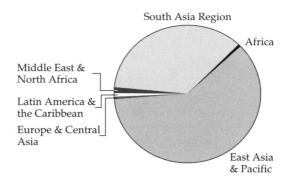

Source: Dixon, Gibbon, and Gulliver 2001.

Irrigation is the cornerstone of agriculture and livelihoods in these areas. Irrigation supports higher levels of production and reduces variability in food crop yields, and it makes it easier for farmers to diversify into growing higher-value products. Although there is wide variation among regions of the world where irrigation is important, irrigated areas are relatively well provisioned with communications, power, and transport systems as well as public social services.

The green revolution transformed agriculture in these areas. Farming systems have become technologically intensive, featuring improved plant varieties, improved animal breeds, and high levels of purchased inputs. The bulk of production is intended for the market. Rice and wheat are the single most important crops. Public policy has widely promoted their production for food security, both directly (e.g., through price supports and input subsidies) and indirectly (through agricultural research biased in favor of cereal crops). After initial success with cereal production, some public support has shifted to cash crops, such as cotton and oilseeds, which have expanded rapidly in many systems. More recently, increasing demand for meat and milk has caused rapid growth in commercial livestock production. Off-farm income typically makes a large contribution to total household income (often up to 40 percent). Demand is stimulated by rising farm incomes, high population density, and proximity to towns and urban areas where employment opportunities exist.

The green revolution caused poverty to decline rapidly in these areas as farm incomes rose, food prices fell, and employment opportunities expanded. Now the links between agricultural growth and poverty reduction have become less direct. Farm mechanization has reduced employment opportunities for landless laborers. Liberalized trade policies influence food prices far more than increased crop productivity. Population growth has caused farms to become smaller and more fragmented, with the result that most farms in densely populated areas cover less than one hectare. Rapid industrialization and urbanization cause agriculture to compete more directly with other sectors for land (as urban areas expand), labor (as wage rates rise in the nonfarm sector), and water (as urban use increases).

In the past, most governments protected, subsidized, taxed, supported, regulated, and generally intervened in these highly productive agricultural systems. The public sector assumed roles that corresponded to the private sector (through parastatals, for example). It neglected some of its public functions, such as land administration and the development of infrastructure. High input subsidies, especially for fertilizers, power, and water, have outlived their original purpose of promoting the use of new technology. Now they foster an inappropriate and often excessive use of inputs that is increasing water pollution, soil erosion, and the loss of biodiversity. Despite substantial liberalization in some countries (e.g., Bangladesh, Pakistan, and Vietnam), the pace of policy reform in others has been very slow for agriculture, even relative to other sectors in the same country (e.g., India).

Looking to the next 10–20 years, it seems likely that the cost of agricultural labor will rise significantly, with a corresponding increase in demand for labor-saving technologies. In areas where mechanization and agricultural intensification are already well underway, the labor force will begin to decline. Opportunities for farm consolidation will grow, but governments will confront the enormous challenge of managing the rate at which a largely unskilled labor force leaves agriculture.

Strategic Investments and Policies

Against this background, what are the most strategic investments and policies for high-potential irrigated areas? Although growth in demand for traditional food crops has slowed significantly, the bulk of demand will probably still have to be met through domestic production. For large Asian countries it simply may not be feasible to import large volumes of food staples from world markets without substantially increasing world prices. Governments will need to support increased public investments in agricultural R&D to improve the productivity and profitability of staple crop production. A priority is to overcome barriers to higher rice and wheat yields without compromising the natural resource base. Simply applying higher levels of inputs will not do the job. The returns to greater input use are declining in many systems, and further intensification in these areas will exact a heavy toll on the environment.

Although some irrigated systems still have scope to intensify production in environmentally appropriate ways, the most important strategies for future growth and poverty reduction are *diversification* of on-farm and off-farm income (figure 5.2) and *exiting* from agriculture in the most highly populated areas. As noted in chapter 2, demand patterns are changing as incomes grow, cities expand, and markets and trade are increasingly liberalized. As these trends continue, they will provide huge opportunities for producers to diversify into higher value products, including fruits, vegetables, livestock, aquaculture, and associated livestock feeds and forages. The opportunities and potential for off-farm income will also grow. Diversification will present new opportunities for adding value to agricultural production, and industrialization will create employment opportunities that spill into rural areas.

Adjusting to changing market structures and enhancing private sector investment: Urbanization and diversification are associated with changes in the way food is processed and distributed at the industry

Figure 5.2 The Relative Weight of Strategic Options in High-Potential Areas

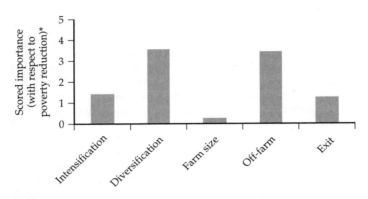

Source: Expert judgment based on Dixon, Gibbon, and Gulliver 2001.
* Scores add to 10.

level. A range of institutional mechanisms and relationships can help private enterprises to join forces and improve information flows, reduce transactions costs, and add value. These include joint ventures, contract farming, vertical integration, and clustering. Producer organizations are likely to play an important role in all of these relationships (box 5.2).

Getting policies right will be critical to ensuring that incentives favor diversification and sustainable agricultural practices. To complement the effects of policy, institutions must be formed or adapted to expand the private sector's role in farm diversification and concurrent development of the nonfarm sector. These institutions will need to provide the appropriate investment climate while ensuring due regard for social equity, empowerment, and environmental sustainability. *Key public sector institutional changes, reforms, and investments required to provide such an environment are:*

- completing the liberalization of market and trade policy, reforming subsidy policies, and dismantling remaining parastatals;
- introducing market risk management mechanisms, such as forward contracts and futures markets;
- developing financial systems for savings, capital redistribution, and risk management;

**Box 5.2 Smallholders and Agribusiness: Contract
Production in Northern Thailand**

In the San Sei district of northern Thailand, small-scale farmers (with
fields averaging 1 hectare) have developed a sustainable rice-potato production system, which they have extended to include new marketing
arrangements. National legislation has promoted the production of high-
quality, value-added products for export through cooperation between
industrial firms, farmers, and financial institutions. At the community
level, the efforts of local officers were central to initiating relationships
and coordinating contracts between firms and farmers. These local efforts
built conditions of trust that had the broader effect of supporting the
entire industry.

Farmers found that growing processing potatoes under contract with
companies and producing cooking potatoes for the domestic market
helped to spread risk and prevent overdependence on one partner. The
Potato Growers Cooperative has been effective in managing the supply
and therefore the price of cooking potatoes, and it has improved farmers'
access to services and resources. Contract farming has helped promote
the production of a quality product in assured quantities. However, the
development and acceptance of formal, modern contractual arrangements
has been a long process. In northern Thailand, it has taken at least
30 years.

Source: Gypmantasiri, Sriboonchitta, and Wiboonpongse 2001 in Vorley 2001.

- supporting infrastructure for irrigation (mostly rehabilitation), markets
  (e.g., cold chains, port infrastructure), and information and communications;
- supporting capacity building for businesses to conform to market
  grades and standards and for public organizations to regulate and cer-
  tify food quality and safety; and
- issuing appropriate contract, employment, competition, and investment laws.

*Agricultural innovation and information systems to share and use
knowledge more effectively:* With land and water becoming scarce, diversification and productivity growth will be knowledge-intensive
processes, and producers will require more market-oriented agricultural
innovation systems to supply new technologies and information. The
private sector must play a central role in these innovation systems, but to
do this imports of technology must be liberalized, and appropriate

incentives must be available in the form of intellectual property rights and a business-friendly investment climate. The public sector must focus on strategic research and certain public good areas, such as natural resource management and the development of environmentally friendly technologies (e.g., integrated pest management). A major question for public research systems is how to sharply upgrade their capacity and effectiveness to meet these new demands (box 5.3).

Box 5.3 China: Reforming Agricultural Research Systems for Market-Oriented Agriculture

Since the 1980s, outdated research practices, overstaffed institutes, duplication of efforts, and underpaid researchers have reduced the effectiveness of China's agricultural research system. Recent reforms have aimed at making the national agricultural research system internationally competitive, state-of-the-art, and merit-based to meet the needs of a market-oriented economy. Research activities have been separated into those that have commercial potential and those that do not.

About one-third of the research institutes are being privatized (e.g., plant breeding for commercial crops). Another third, with the best scientists, is being upgraded through salary incentives, improved budgets, and new facilities and equipment to conduct public goods research of a strategic nature. The remaining third will be made redundant. Competitive grant funding (for operating costs and infrastructure) is being increased significantly, with a larger share of funds allocated to high-technology research. Important lessons include:

- The design and implementation of reforms are usually much more difficult than envisaged. In particular, successful commercialization requires more time and effort than expected.
- Reforms have winners and losers. The vision of the goals and desired results must be endorsed by all stakeholders, and a continuous effort must be made to keep everyone committed to reaching the goals.
- Significant budget increases are needed initially for reform, to attract the best scientists and conduct research that leads to sustained productivity.
- Successful commercialization often depends on broader reforms outside of the research system, such as seed industry reform and the transfer of welfare burdens (e.g., retirement) to a general social security system.
- Only a dynamic and visionary set of leaders can successfully champion reforms to internal stakeholders (i.e., institute staff and clients) and policy makers.

Source: Huang et al. 2002.

Improving the efficiency of land and water markets: In many areas, production cannot become more efficient unless land is consolidated. When land holdings are fragmented and divided into uneconomically small plots, they present a considerable obstacle to improving the productivity of land and labor. In densely populated areas, efforts to consolidate land must be complemented by efforts to help people leave the farm. The modernization of land administration systems should receive high priority in many of these areas to permit efficient land markets to develop. Opportunities to expand irrigated area are limited. Efforts must focus instead on rehabilitating and modifying irrigation systems so that water is used more efficiently and distributed more equitably. New investments must focus on devising and disseminating appropriate technologies to manage water, reducing environmental damage, and promoting water markets so that water can be priced and allocated to

---

Box 5.4 Mali: Success in Combining Policy Reforms, Institutional Reforms, and Strategic Investments

The Office du Niger in Mali, an irrigation system regarded for many years as a bottomless pit for public funds, is now seen as a success story. Created during colonial times to produce cotton, the Office abandoned cotton for rice in the 1950s because of problems with waterlogged soils. With support from the World Bank, the Netherlands, France, and others, the Office restructured in the 1980s, changing its organizational structure as well as its technical activities. Paddy processing and marketing functions were privatized. Current activities focus on such essential functions as providing water services, planning, and maintaining infrastructure. Improved water delivery and land leveling enabled the adoption of rice transplanting methods and high-yielding varieties, increasing paddy yields from 1.5 to 6 tons per hectare.

Although no formal water user associations exist, farmers elect delegates to represent them on joint committees that determine how water fees will be used. Each committee, which covers about 5,000 to 8,000 hectares, decides on the annual maintenance program, budget, and procurement, while day-to-day management remains the responsibility of the Office. This approach matches the capacity level of the farmers, and it may be a suitable model for other low-income countries with a low level of literacy.

Source: Couture and Lavigne 2000.

reflect its true costs and benefits. Mali's improved water services and the subsequent remarkable increase in paddy yields illustrate the importance of making strategic investments in concert with market-oriented policies and institutional innovation (box 5.4).

Managing the pollution effects of intensive production: Agricultural intensification poses major challenges for managing waste from livestock production and aquaculture, as well as pollution from agricultural chemicals. Developing policies and decision-support tools, building capacity, raising awareness, enforcing policies and regulations, and facilitating cooperation among institutions will be important in managing these externalities. In many instances, regional cooperation and coordination is especially important to share what is learned at the national level and to foster other synergies (e.g., cost-savings for the development of policy tools, given that the impacts are not always confined to specific countries) (box 5.5).

Off-farm employment opportunities must grow: Off-farm employment is vital to the strategy for these areas. People will need more remunerative

---

Box 5.5 East Asia: Drowning in a Sea of Livestock Waste?

The South China Sea is a locally, regionally, and globally significant body of water that is surrounded by countries experiencing rapid population and economic growth. The great biological richness of the sea and coastal areas are seriously threatened by land-based pollution. This region is the most important livestock-producing region in the world. Roughly 80 percent of the total recent increase in livestock production stems from intensive production enterprises, mostly located near urban centers in coastal areas. Pig production alone is the largest livestock-based source of water, air, and soil pollution in the region. China, Thailand, and Vietnam all recognize the detrimental environmental impact of exponential growth in intensive livestock production and have started developing appropriate regulations and other measures. These measures alone will not solve the problem, and they have been weakened through poor enforcement.

Under a Global Environmental Facility (GEF) grant, implemented by the World Bank in close collaboration with FAO/LEAD (the Livestock, Environment and Development Initiative), a pilot program is testing national incentive and regulatory systems to improve the geographical distribution of intensive production units, prevent further pollution, and, at the watershed level, mitigate the effects of pollution.

Source: World Bank internal documents.

employment, and rapid growth in the nonfarm sector will increase demand for labor. Growth in the farm sector can spur growth in the nonfarm sector by increasing the demand for labor to process and package food and other products. New technologies will reduce crop losses and increase product quality, which in turn will expand prospects for off-farm employment by making value-adding enterprises and post-harvest management systems more competitive.

Rural people's capacity to earn income off of the farm can be improved by strengthening institutions that facilitate private decision making by reducing risk, increasing mobility, minimizing barriers to entry, improving education and infrastructure, ensuring fairness and transparency in the conduct of public agencies, and helping the poor identify opportunities and access assets.

Entry Points for Public Policy

For high-potential areas, with their high population density, good infrastructure, and rather profitable agriculture, public policy should focus on creating the enabling environment for the private sector. The World Bank's work to support the development of food chains, food safety regulations, and a positive climate for private investment, as well as its growing relationship with the IFC, will continue to broaden the understanding of how to work with private partners to achieve the desired economic and social objectives. Much will also be learned from other donors, such as USAID and French Cooperation. *Support could include:*

- *Analytical work on the remaining policy agenda,* such as on further market and trade liberalization and reduction of subsidies. Irrigated, intensive agriculture prevails mainly in large countries, including China and India, where the World Bank's direct contribution can only be small in comparison with the total development budget. The greatest impact can be achieved by conducting high-quality analyses for the agricultural sector, preferably in close cooperation with national policy institutes.
- *Investments to develop and deliver public goods,* especially investments in research, infrastructure, and human capital. Much has been learned about successfully rehabilitating irrigation schemes, and significant expertise is available in promoting water user associations, which are often critical to success. Lessons that are emerging on how to develop more demand-driven, pluralistic innovation systems will also assist high-potential areas in their goal to diversify agriculture.

- *Continued learning and experimentation* on better ways of supporting growth led by the private sector, including appropriate market regulations and standards.

Agricultural Growth in High- and Medium-Potential Systems with Limited Access to Markets

Of the total agricultural land in developing countries, 27 percent has high or medium agroecological potential but suffers from limited access to markets. This megasystem is especially important in Africa.

Defining Characteristics of the System

The biophysical endowments of these systems, especially their good climate and soils, give them great potential to increase agricultural production, but this potential has been frustrated by barriers to transportation and communication. Agriculture in these areas encompasses mixed maize farming systems in eastern and southern Africa, extensive mixed farming systems in Latin America, and rainfed systems in central and southern India (figure 5.3; annex 1). Because areas with good agricultural potential but poor access to markets are much more critical for Sub-Saharan Africa than for any other region (58 percent of the total population and 60 percent of the agricultural population reside there), the discussion that follows will be oriented toward Africa.

Figure 5.3 High-Potential Low-Access Areas: Agricultural Population Distribution by Region

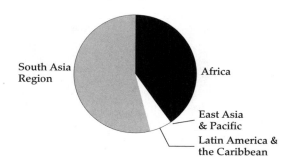

Source: Dixon, Gibbon, and Gulliver 2001.

Rainfall and temperatures vary widely in these areas, but typically they allow a relatively long growing period (e.g., 120–180 days in the cereal-root crop mixed farming systems of Africa) that can support a diverse range of agricultural production systems. The constraint that distinguishes these systems is their limited access to markets, caused by one or any combination of three factors:

- producers are isolated by long distances or difficult topography from densely populated areas with large, active markets;
- inadequate infrastructure and support services, such as roads, communication systems, and extension services; and
- weak purchasing power and demand in the markets themselves.

High transportation costs, often exacerbated by the existence of transport monopolies, discourage the commercial production of bulky products such as cereals. Lengthy transit times limit sales of agricultural products to nonperishable commodities. Despite the relatively good climatic conditions characteristic of these systems, they do suffer from frequent and severe climatic events. The effects of these events are compounded by poor infrastructure and weak financial systems.

Under these conditions, agriculture is oriented toward the production of staples to support household food security, sometimes complemented by the production of nonperishable cash crops such as cotton and coffee. Soils are generally resilient and capable of supporting a range of intensive production enterprises, but restricted access to inputs and increasing population pressure are degrading the land, which also suffers the effects of overgrazing, erosion, and deforestation. In Africa in particular, very low use of inorganic fertilizers, coupled with the shorter fallow periods that result from growing population pressure on the land, has resulted in serious soil mining and degradation.

Livestock are generally an important part of the farming system: animals can literally be walked to market, and livestock sales can provide a major part of the farm family's cash income. Livestock production is still heavily constrained by the high disease pressure on animals and people alike (e.g., sleeping sickness and river blindness in Africa).

Poverty in these areas is generally high and typically associated with vulnerability to climatic disasters, inadequate access to services, and the declining productive capacity of natural resources. Emigration of younger people results in an aging population, a high proportion of female-headed households, and high dependency ratios, which are all the more common where HIV/AIDS is devastating farm populations. Nonfarm income is usually important, especially in the dry season and from seasonal work outside the local area.

Strategic Investments and Policies

Because the good biophysical endowments of these systems favor the production of a much broader range of agricultural products, intensification and diversification are the two major strategies (figure 5.4), although the expansion of cultivated area will still be an important strategy where land prices are low (McIntire, Bourzat, and Pingali 1992).

Intensification and diversification require substantial public and private investments to increase productivity per worker and output per unit of land farmed. A high priority is to improve the productivity, quality, and seasonal availability of food crops, because households depend so heavily on producing crops for home consumption, and because food markets are poorly developed. A corresponding priority is to raise farm profitability by improving access to markets for inputs and outputs, as well as access to technologies that can enhance the productivity of labor (where land scarcity is not a main constraint).

As the productivity and profitability of food crop production increases, priority should be given to diversification. By strengthening links to market outlets (for example, through investments in roads and information systems), farmers can produce more low-volume, higher-value, nonperishable crop and livestock products for the market. Further diversification to products requiring more inputs, processing, and handling will present opportunities for developing the nonfarm economy.[5]

Figure 5.4 The Relative Weight of Strategic Options in High-Potential Low-Access Areas

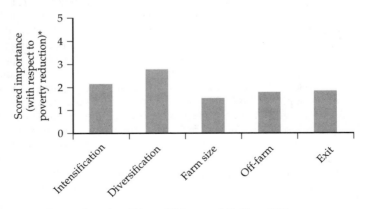

Source: Expert judgment based on Dixon, Gibbon, and Gulliver 2001.
* Scores add to 10.

Although most policy reform, institution building, and investments are all relevant for this system, "getting markets right" is especially important. *A number of measures will contribute to this goal.*

Investments in physical infrastructure for improved market links: In most areas, investment in infrastructure is the first step. The choice of investment and financing responsibilities often can be devolved to lower levels using participatory, demand-driven approaches (chapter 4). Overall, it is important that efforts to improve infrastructure occur within a national framework that captures demand and supply links across sectors, and synergies among rural sectors.

Investments to support institutional innovations for market development: Market development requires support for key market institutions. Innovative approaches to stimulating market development, such as targeted vouchers to obtain inputs, have been piloted in Malawi with donor support (see chapter 3, box 3.9). Support is also needed for institutional innovations that facilitate coordination along the supply chain, including contract farming, outgrower schemes (in which an agribusiness complements its supplies through arrangements with surrounding smallholders), and farmers' and traders' associations (see discussions of export

---

Box 5.6 Small African Seed Enterprises

The recent emergence of small seed enterprises in Africa illustrates the possible sources of skills and resources that can support seed enterprise development.

Uganda: Harvest Farm Seeds. A grain trading company in Kampala became involved in procuring grain suitable for seed for relief operations in neighboring countries. With this experience, it established Harvest Farm Seeds to produce and sell commercial seed of varieties developed by public research organizations. Harvest Farm Seeds still sells most of its inventory to relief organizations, but it is strengthening its marketing network in Uganda and planning to establish its own plant breeding capacity.

Ghana: Seed producers. The collapse of the parastatal Ghana Seed Company in the 1980s left producers without a formal source of seed for maize and cowpeas. A project funded by Sasakawa-Global 2000 approached former contract growers about establishing their own enterprises. The project supervised their seed production, facilitated contacts with local input dealers to purchase and market the seed, coordinated access to public seed processing facilities, and provided seed certification services. A viable private and cooperative seed industry based on small- and medium-size enterprises has been established to serve the needs of many farmers.

Source: World Bank 2004b.

crops from Mali and Guatemala in chapter 3, and artisanal seed systems in box 5.6). Moreover, capacity building is required for regulation and monitoring, which are crucial institutional elements for agricultural markets to function well. It may be necessary to develop official systems of grades and standards and well-functioning market information systems.

Investments in technology to improve profitability: Access to markets must be improved, but so must access to new technologies and advisory services to improve profitability and expand smallholders' awareness of market opportunities. New mechanisms for investing in such services provide funds for producer organizations to contract with service providers (often NGOs) to deliver the required service (box 5.7).

Risk management: To help farmers cope with changing markets and production systems, investments must be made in financial systems for coping with risk (see the detailed discussion in chapter 3 of futures markets, insurance schemes based on weather indices, warehouse receipt systems, commodity exchanges, and social safety nets).

Land policy changes: Increasing population pressure and commercialization are eroding the effectiveness of traditional customary land institutions. Land use in Sub-Saharan Africa is now frequently governed by complex interaction between customary institutions and national law, and uncertainties regarding tenure result in underinvestment and depletion of the natural resource base. Establishing efficient land administration

---

Box 5.7 Senegal Supports a Rigorous and Demand-Driven Research Agenda

The National Agricultural Research Fund (NARF), a legally independent entity, has made it possible to separate the funding of research from the execution of research projects in Senegal. Based on a rigorous screening of proposals, NARF contracts with qualified entities, public and private, to conduct research projects. At the same time, parallel core funding provides government research institutes with funds for infrastructure, training, and strengthening its management capacity. The two separate funding mechanisms (core funding for research institutes and NARF-contracted research) guarantee that institutional development continues, while funding for operating costs goes directly to researchers working on projects relevant to users, to whom researchers are accountable. Overall, 38 organizations with research capacity, including international organizations (12 percent of projects) and development agencies such as RPOs and NGOs (58 percent of projects), have received funding.

Source: World Bank 2004b.

systems should take a high priority in many of these areas, but familiarity with both customary and formal land law, and the types of local organizations recognized under law, is needed.

Entry Points for Public Policy

With respect to policy and institutional issues, key areas of attention include risk management and product markets. The application of the innovative approaches described in chapters 3 and 4 can be envisaged, although experience with these approaches requires close monitoring, evaluation, and learning before they can be scaled up.

The major challenge for these systems lies in scaling up investments to support market development in the higher potential areas of Africa, where the impacts of externally supported investments often have been disappointing. Sequencing is critically important here to ensure that the forces of production, markets, and technology development work coherently toward successful market development. In addition to the investments described above, attention will have to be given to increasing problems of natural resource degradation, especially strategies to restore soil fertility in Africa and deforested areas in Central and South America. This environmental goal can be reached by continued scaling up of low-input systems, following such models as conservation tillage farming in Brazil (box 5.8).

Box 5.8 Brazil Takes the Long View and Adopts Conservation Tillage Farming

Over the past five years, conservation tillage farming has increased farm incomes in Brazil by 59 percent and maize yields by 20 percent on millions of hectares. Conservation tillage is far from a "quick fix" for sustainability or profitability problems, however. It works through careful, often time-consuming adaptation to local circumstances, and some time must also elapse before the benefits are apparent.

Experience in Paraná, Brazil, illustrates key elements of conservation tillage systems for smallholder maize and bean production: (1) use of animal traction, family labor, and limited use of purchased inputs; (2) special animal-drawn equipment for planting and for managing biomass (crops and crop residues); (3) the use of cover crop management; (4) runoff control with contour bunds built with an animal-drawn moldboard plow; and (5) planting of dwarf elephant grass on contour bunds for livestock feed.

Source: Pieri et al. 2002; World Bank 2004b.

Agricultural Growth and Sustainability in Marginal Drylands

Marginal drylands are sparsely populated and often remote, with highly limited agroecological potential and poor access to markets.[6] These areas are often characterized by extreme poverty.

Defining Characteristics of the System

Marginal dryland areas are distributed relatively evenly throughout the developing world (figure 5.5). Some 2,800 million hectares (about 30 percent of the total land area in developing countries) can be described as marginal drylands, but only 4 percent of this land is cultivated, and only 8 percent of the agricultural population in developing countries lives in these areas.

Farming systems range from the sparsely populated arid and agropastoral millet-sorghum systems of Sub-Saharan Africa to the mixed intensive highlands of the north Andes in Latin America (annex 1). Livestock production is often the most important enterprise, with extensive pastoral systems being the most common.

The rural population consists largely of subsistence-oriented households who lack most types of assets. The incidence and severity of poverty in these areas is generally high and getting worse. Marginalized social groups tend to be concentrated in marginal areas, including indigenous people, refugees, female-headed households, and pastoralists. These

Figure 5.5 Marginal Drylands: Agricultural Population Distribution by Region

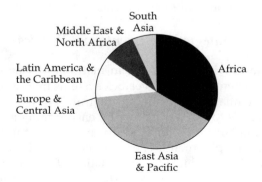

Source: Dixon, Gibbon, and Gulliver 2001.

groups often face discrimination in gaining access to the very limited productive resources, social services, and infrastructure (e.g., schools, drinking water, and health care) in these areas. In sites of higher potential within marginal dryland areas, conflicts persist over land and water resources, fueled by unclear or overlapping ownership and use rights.

Because of high production risks, compounded by the very high cost of importing food, households diversify their sources of income within and outside agriculture. Aside from crop and livestock production, a significant share of household income (anywhere between 20 and 90 percent) is derived from off-farm employment in local services, construction, handicrafts, and other small-scale manufacturing and service activities. Remittances from seasonal migration have become vital for coping with poverty in many areas.

Despite the noted adaptation and resilience of annual vegetation in arid lands (Scoones 1994), traditional strategies may no longer be sufficient for coping with the environmental conditions in these areas. The inherent fragility of the resource base in dryland areas means that even small increases in population pressure can render land use practices unsustainable and provoke irreversible environmental degradation. Major environmental problems include overgrazing of pasturelands and the encroachment of arable farming into areas unsuited for agriculture. Farming in unsuitable areas depletes and erodes soils and reduces biodiversity, all of which limit the land's long-term production potential and raise production risks (for example, by prolonging the duration and severity of droughts—typically the greatest source of vulnerability in these areas).

The natural resource base (and its low production potential) often cannot support the current population. In this classical "poverty trap," the risk posed by systemic food shortages as well as seasonal hunger forces households to allocate their resources in less than optimal ways, aggravates land degradation, and further escalates food insecurity.

Strategic Investments and Policies

Strategies for improving livelihoods in marginal dryland areas involve improving the current crop and livestock systems in locations with somewhat higher potential and sustaining them in the rest. Over the longer term, the strategy is to exit agriculture by encouraging migration as well as alternative, nonfarm uses for land (to conserve natural resources and promote off-farm employment). These strategies involve extreme changes for rural people. They will need a combination of risk management at the farm level, safety nets at the household level, and other forms of transitional support.

Exit from agriculture is by far the most important strategy for dryland marginal areas, followed by growth in off-farm employment growth (figure 5.6). Because exit is a longer-term objective, especially in poorer countries where opportunities to participate in nonagricultural labor markets are fairly limited, an intermediate step is to reduce poverty by developing those agricultural systems that can be viable. Improvements at the farm level should help rural households enhance food security, conserve natural resources, and if possible enter markets for selected products in which they have a comparative advantage (e.g., arid zone fruits and nuts, spices, honey, herbs, agroforestry, and small livestock). Given the critical role of livestock, efforts to reduce the effects of interannual and interseasonal variation in feed availability through strategic fodder production, range management, and livestock marketing are often critical. Where improvements of the asset base are feasible, for example through small-scale irrigation, they can transform livelihoods.

Recent successful experiences in dryland areas illustrate the potential for sustaining and even increasing the productivity of arable cropping (table 5.2). These successes generally combine elements of water conservation or small-scale irrigation, management of natural resources held in common, and CDD grants to communities for small-scale infrastructure and income-generating activities, both on and off the farm.

Institutions for collective action and empowerment: Subsistence-oriented households can significantly improve their options and assets through

Figure 5.6 The Relative Weight of Strategic Options in Marginal Drylands

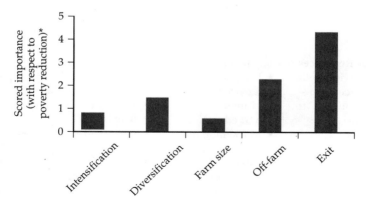

Source: Expert judgment based on Dixon, Gibbon, and Gulliver 2001.
* Scores add to 10.

Table 5.2 Recent World Bank–Financed Development Projects in Dryland Areas

Project and type of marginal area	What was supported	Changes/impacts
Irrigation		
Nigeria: Fadama Projects (1993 to present) Investment: US$104 million	• Small-scale irrigation with tube-wells • Farmers' organizations • Adaptive research and extension • Rural roads, storage, and marketing	• 100,000 hectares of irrigation brought into production • Increased returns per hectare from 65 percent for vegetables to over 300 percent for wheat/rice; increased farm incomes up to 90 percent • Average return of 40 percent to investment • *But:* Increased conflicts between different users (arable farmers, pastoralists, fishers)
Community-Driven Development		
Brazil: Northeast Rural Development Program and the Poverty Alleviation Program (1993 to present) Investment: US$800 million to 2001	• Capacity development for community associations • Grants averaging US$26,000 for infrastructure (water, electricity) and productive activities • Links to and supports local government organizations	• 44,000 subprojects funded involving 7.5 million people • Reduced cost of providing local infrastructure and services • Typical productive subproject yields annual income of over US$20,000 with economic rate of return to productive subprojects from 30 to 60 percent
Natural Resources Management		
Kenya: Arid Lands Resources Management (1997 to present) Investment: US$25 million	• Early warning systems for drought • Human health and education • Marketing and infrastructure for livestock • Water supply • Animal production and health services	• Improved early warning systems for drought • 1,200 subprojects with 180,000 beneficiaries • Improved access to water and health facilities • *But:* Lack of impact on range rehabilitation

Table 5.2 *(Continued)*

Project and type of marginal area	What was supported	Changes/impacts
Watershed Management		
China: Loess Plateau Watershed Rehabilitation (1995 to present) Investment: US$97 million	• Land rehabilitation including terracing and forests • Training, adaptive research, and extension	• Over one million farmers participated, to be scaled up to three million by 2005 • 90,000 hectares of terraces and reduction in sediment inflow to Yellow River • Farm income per capita rose by 343 percent • Economic return of 29 percent

Source: Kelley and Byerlee 2003.

stronger local institutions, networks, and organizations that they can use to mobilize their very scarce resources and link to external networks. Because communities in dryland areas are often excluded from political processes, and there is limited potential for private sector involvement, community and producer organizations may be the primary means of widening access to services and markets. These organizations can assume some of the functions of the public sector by investing in local infrastructure, giving the rural poor a voice in political processes and in demanding services, and developing income-generating activities.

To effectively fulfill these functions, collective organizations must often strengthen their internal governance and accountability, information systems, capacity to articulate members' needs, and ability to negotiate for technical and managerial support. They must also work within a framework that ensures inclusiveness (box 5.9).

These organizations are often supported through CDD approaches that make it possible to develop community-led initiatives, collectively manage natural resources, and establish participatory approaches to provide services. Although the CDD approach has shown potential to reach isolated populations in relatively marginal agroecological zones, community groups have proved generally less effective at managing common property natural resources than at working toward enhancing economic benefits (box 5.10). The World Bank has also supported pastoral associations in West Africa with generally good success in the area of service delivery, but it has been difficult to sustain the resource management activities of these groups once projects have ended. The biggest challenge—yet unsolved—is to find ways to scale up successful local experiences in these very diverse and often remote areas.

Box 5.9 India: Designing a Socially Inclusive Watershed Project

One of four key goals of the Karnataka Watershed Development Project in India is to reach marginalized and vulnerable groups. The project, which required the development and implementation of a Tribals and Vulnerable Groups Development Plan, focused on watersheds in Karnataka's rainfed areas where some of the poorest populations resided. These people, who subsisted on the most slender resources, included scheduled castes, other disenfranchised groups, the landless, and people living below the poverty line. Project implementation committees are composed of various groups with interests in the outcome. At least 50 percent of the executive committee is female, and some are from scheduled tribes and other vulnerable groups. Nongovernmental organizations are intensively involved in building stakeholders' capacity in forming and sustaining collective organizations, integrated watershed planning and implementing activities in a participatory way, and monitoring and evaluating progress throughout the life of the project.

Source: World Bank internal documents.

Sustainable land use practices to use scarce resources wisely: Without more sustainable land use practices, people in marginal drylands will be hard pressed to make the best use of scarce water resources, reduce soil erosion and water runoff, and conserve natural pastures and vegetation. Success in various resource management initiatives illustrates that well-designed and targeted initiatives can reverse resource degradation and/or improve productivity. Woodlot planting in sparsely populated areas can reduce the use of dung and crop residues for fuel and offer viable income opportunities. Hedgerow intercropping, silvopastoral systems, and relay cropping are all productive agroforestry systems with considerable potential for scaling up in low-access areas.

Environmental services with social and economic benefits: The conservation of biodiversity, an important asset in marginal drylands, is particularly challenging yet potentially rewarding. Indigenous ethnic groups have extensive knowledge and skills relating to plant and animal biodiversity. This diversity is important not only for its biological and ecological functions, but also for its economic value in food, medicinal, and industrial uses. A social and economic challenge is to design contracts for using (or domesticating) biodiversity with sound mechanisms for sharing benefits fairly among stakeholders. One way to enhance biodiversity is by

---

Box 5.10 Zimbabwe: Uneven Benefits from Community Management of Natural Resources

The Communal Areas Management Program for Indigenous Resources is a rural development and conservation initiative in Zimbabwe that seeks to provide rural people the authority to manage and benefit from their natural resources. The program has decentralized decision making and devolved responsibilities for managing resources to the local level, thereby passing financial incentives for conservation management to local communities. In some areas, devolution of power successfully ended dependence on central institutions and brought about self-reliance and self-sufficiency. In areas where the control of natural resources and their economic benefits were retained at the district council level or higher, local communities were left frustrated and powerless, provoking misunderstandings, hostility toward the program, and continued illegal poaching and encroachment into wildlife areas.

Source: Grimble and Laidlaw 2002.

---

integrating wildlife management with livestock production to bridge conflicting interests. In arid and semi-arid landscapes, although the profitability for pure game ranching is limited, mixed game and livestock ranching can provide higher and less volatile profits than livestock production alone, and can simultaneously reduce land degradation and enhance biodiversity.

Small-scale irrigation has potential for scaling up: Small-scale irrigation projects have been successful in many settings, including Africa, and there is considerable potential for scaling up these approaches. The *fadama* (valley bottom) projects in northern Nigeria have transformed the livelihoods of about half a million people, even through conflicts over land and water use between arable farmers, pastoralists, and fishers in fadama areas remain a major concern. Using small diesel pumps, farmers can grow onions, tomatoes, and chilies in the dry season, and these vegetables have replaced the traditional staples of sorghum and millet as the main source of household income. Similar programs using hand pumps have succeeded elsewhere. Often irrigation initiatives can be incorporated effectively into watershed management approaches in which collective action harmonizes the use of soil, water, and vegetation in the watershed to increase productivity and conserve resources, as in Sukhomajri village in India (box 5.11).

Livestock and pastoral development to improve food security: Livestock are often the key to improving food security and reducing poverty in marginal drylands. For livestock producers to gain access to regional

---

Box 5.11 India: Sharing the Costs and Benefits of Watershed Management

In Sukhomajri village, India, a project provided irrigation water from a small runoff pond. Landless families used the pond's catchment area for grazing, but the resulting lack of vegetative cover caused erosion that threatened the pond with siltation. To resolve this problem, villagers proposed that landless families receive rights to irrigation water in exchange for eliminating grazing in the catchment area. Irrigators pay for the water they use, and proceeds are distributed equally among households regardless of their landholding status.

Source: World Bank internal documents.

---

markets, they require access to veterinary services, animal health products, and more developed market channels, including provisions for compliance with sanitary standards (to minimize the risks of spreading contagious diseases) and food safety (processing) standards. Another important element in developing sustainable and productive livestock systems is to provide improved feed from higher potential sites in dryland areas, such as valley bottoms or spring and autumn pastures in Central Asia. There is now conclusive evidence that migratory pastoral systems, which take advantage of different landscapes during different seasons, are the most ecological and economically efficient systems, and strategies to settle migratory pastoralists generally worsen environmental degradation and social deprivation.

Reducing vulnerability to change: Safety nets may be appropriate in certain circumstances. These measures could include food grants or vouchers, to ensure that people attain a minimum standard of living (especially when there is a drought); one-time transfer payments, to enable farmers to fund their transition out of agriculture and into other employment; and permanent transfers, such as payments for environmental services. Improving farmers' capacity to manage production risks is often a critical step toward sustainable and profitable agriculture. The case of northern Kenya demonstrates that an effective drought management system can give vulnerable populations in drought-prone areas the means of managing risks and improving their livelihoods at an acceptable cost (see chapter 3, box 3.17).

Investments in producers' capacity to prepare for and respond to drought should provide for drought preparedness, early warning systems, better drought management capabilities, and assistance to recover from drought. Group organizations are often an effective vehicle for developing capacity to manage production risks and reduce vulnerability to disasters.

Entry Points for Public Policy

In marginal drylands, more than in the other agricultural systems discussed in this chapter, widespread poverty and the predominance of goods held in common justify public support from the World Bank and other international donors. The main policy issues are to bring marginal areas and their often minority populations into the policy dialogue (chapter 6) and to design safety nets that concentrate on preventing disasters rather than creating dependency on food aid, without crowding out local initiatives.

On the investment side, in spite of the perceived low potential for development in these areas, as shown by successful experience (table 5.2), much can be done. In pastoral areas, the World Bank is involved in a new generation of projects in China, Ethiopia, Kenya, and Mongolia, often in collaboration with other donors such as the International Fund for Agricultural Development (IFAD) and DFID. Although they differ in design, all of these projects have strong community development and risk management aspects that pave the way for better access to markets.

Good opportunities for increased impact and poverty reduction exist in watershed development in areas that have somewhat higher potential. Varying combinations of decentralized decision making on investments for erosion control, reforestation, feed production, small-scale irrigation, and market development have all proven to be successful entry points. These higher-potential areas within arid environments are often the part of the ecosystem that is essential to the livelihoods of everyone throughout the entire system.

Increasing the Impact of Investments in Diverse Agricultural Contexts

As this chapter has shown, it is possible to classify agricultural systems based on broad similarities and then identify which strategies and policies are most likely to promote economic growth and reduce poverty in each one. The need to tailor approaches to particular contexts adds an additional level of complexity to choices surrounding agricultural investments, but investments are essential if agriculture is to help countries progress toward the MDGs. The next chapter will look at ways of improving the quality and impact of investments in agriculture, especially through innovative partnerships and new areas of investment that are more consistent with a stronger market orientation in developing country agriculture.

Annex 1 Major Farming Systems That Fall within Each of the Three Megasystems

Major systems in irrigated high-potential areas

System	Region	Land area (% of region)	Agricultural population (% of region)	Principal livelihoods
Lowland rice	East Asia and Pacific	12	42	Rice, maize, pulses, sugarcane, oilseeds, vegetables, livestock, aquaculture, off-farm work
Temperate mixed	East Asia and Pacific	6	14	Wheat, maize, pulses, oilseeds, livestock, off-farm work
Rice	South Asia	7	17	Wetland rice (both seasons), vegetables, legumes, off-farm activities
Rice-wheat	South Asia	19	33	Irrigated rice, wheat, vegetables, livestock (including dairy), off-farm activities

Major systems in high- and medium-potential areas with limited access to markets

System	Region	Land area (% of region)	Agricultural population (% of region)	Principal livelihoods
Highland mixed	South Asia	12	7	Cereals, livestock, horticulture, seasonal migration
Rainfed mixed	South Asia	29	30	Cereals, legumes, fodder crops, livestock, off-farm activities
Cereal-livestock (*campos*)	Latin America and the Caribbean	5	6	Rice and livestock
Cereal-root crop mixed	Sub-Saharan Africa	13	15	Maize, sorghum, millet, cassava, yams, legumes, cattle
Maize mixed	Sub-Saharan Africa	10	15	Maize, tobacco, cotton, cattle, goats, poultry, off-farm work

Major systems in marginal drylands

System	Region	Land area (% of region)	Agricultural population (% of region)	Principal livelihoods
Temperate mixed (*pampas*)	America and the Caribbean	5	6	Livestock, wheat, soybean
Root–tuber	East Asia and Pacific	2	<1	Root crops (yam, taro, sweet potato), vegetables, fruits, livestock (pigs and cattle), off-farm work
Highland perennial	Sub-Saharan Africa	1	8	Banana, plantain, enset, coffee, cassava, sweet potato, beans, cereals, livestock, poultry, off-farm work
High-altitude mixed (Central Andes)	America and the Caribbean	6	7	Tubers, sheep, grains, llamas, vegetables, off-farm work
Agro-pastoral millet/sorghum	Sub-Saharan Africa	8	8	Sorghum, pearl millet, pulses, sesame, cattle, sheep, goats, poultry, off-farm work
Highland extensive mixed	East Asia and Pacific	5	4	Upland rice, pulses, maize, oil seeds, fruits, forest products, livestock, off-farm work
Dryland mixed	Middle East and North Africa	4	14	Cereals, sheep, off-farm work
Pastoral	Sub-Saharan Africa	14	7	Cattle, camels, sheep, goats, remittances
Sparse (arid)	East Asia and Pacific	20	2	Local grazing where water available, off-farm work

Source: Dixon, Gibbon, and Gulliver 2001.

Annex 2 Strategies and Priorities to Promote Economic Growth and Reduce Poverty in Three Megasystems

Irrigated high-potential areas

Strategy	Priorities for policy and institutional change	Priorities for public investment
Diversification and exit (off-farm employment)	• Liberal trade policy in conjunction with appropriate competition, employment, and contract law to facilitate trade • Strong regulatory framework for food safety and for pest and disease control • Efficient land administration, property rights, and intellectual property rights to induce investment and innovation (including land tenure arrangements to transfer land more efficiently and consolidate landholdings to benefit from economies of scale) • Reform irrigation systems and develop water markets • Foster producer organizations to engage in new supply chain arrangements (including contract farming) and obtain financial services that enable diversification (e.g., credit and risk management instruments) • Support innovation systems that will supply new technologies and information, especially for nontraditional, high-value products, but also for breaking yield barriers in staple crops • Environmental policies to manage pollution from intensive systems • Policies that improve the mobility and efficiency of labor (e.g., education, communication and transport infrastructure, labor laws)	• Public good infrastructure and knowledge to (1) promote private investment in marketing, storage, processing, R&D, and extension; and (2) enable producers to diversify and move toward the primary production of tradable, high-value products • Capacity building for businesses to conform to market grades and standards and for the public sector to regulate food safety • Rehabilitation and maintenance of irrigation systems to improve water allocation and water use efficiency • Investment in human capital to develop the entrepreneurial and technical capacity to pursue market-oriented opportunities for diversification • Capacity building to prepare and enforce environmental regulations

High- and medium-potential systems with limited access to markets

Strategy	Priorities for policy and institutional change	Priorities for public investment
Intensification and diversification	• Policies that encourage private sector investment in infrastructure that improves access to markets (or possibly private sector/civil society provision of publicly funded infrastructure) • Reform of policies that currently inhibit market development or reduce market efficiency (e.g., privatization of parastatals, reduction of subsidies) • Action by producer groups to fill gaps in public investment, achieve economies of scale, and improve bargaining power • Institutions to finance seasonal and initial investments by farmers and rural enterprises • Institutional innovation to stimulate market development, including contract farming and targeted voucher systems • Policies enabling equitable land access • Institutional mechanisms to manage risk (e.g., insurance schemes), promote diversification, and encourage participation in off-farm employment	• Infrastructure (roads and communication) to improve access to input and output markets, both directly and via community organizations • Provision and possibly delivery of technology and market information systems to help link production to markets • Public investments in land distribution and titling as appropriate

Annex 2 *(Continued)*

Marginal drylands

Strategy	Priorities for policy and institutional change	Priorities for public investment
Exit and off-farm employment	• Institutions for collective action, sustained by a policy environment that enables group organization to function (including the decentralization of policy processes) • Policies (including land policy) that give people equitable access to assets, as well as institutional arrangements such as herders' associations to manage common pool resources (e.g., pastures and watersheds) when private ownership is not desirable or possible • Institutions (e.g., safety nets and transfers) and organizations (e.g., community groups) to help people manage vulnerability • Policies and regulations to provide incentives for sustainable natural resource management and the provision of environmental services	• Human capital development (education and training) to enable migration • Community-driven development initiatives to manage natural resources and generate income • Environmental service and other permanent or one-time transfers or payments • Investments in small-scale irrigation for farmers and adequate access to resources for pastoralists • Drought management and preparedness mechanisms, coupled with response systems

Source: Authors.

6

Getting Agriculture Back on the Development Agenda

In this chapter

Agricultural investments must yield the greatest possible impact and promote greater awareness of agriculture's effectiveness in achieving the Millennium Development Goals (MDGs). *Four interlocking actions will improve the quality and impact of investments in agricultural development:*

- *Improving agricultural stakeholders' participation in the policy dialogue:* Four key steps will ensure that stakeholders are well prepared and well represented to gain higher priority for agriculture in policy and investment decisions: (1) strengthening capacity in ministries of agriculture and related ministries; (2) supporting producer and processor organizations; (3) supporting the preparation of national agricultural strategies; and (4) informing policy makers through good analytical studies.
- *Tailoring proposed investments to prevailing financing instruments:* Agricultural investments must be adapted to take advantage of the increasing array of financing instruments and financing partnerships that is available. Examples are given of the different financing instruments that are used as an innovation moves from the experimental stage to piloting, introducing and disseminating good practices, scaling up, and on to widespread adoption.
- *Enhancing the impact of agricultural investments:* Much can be achieved by reducing project preparation costs, ensuring that programmatic funding provides continuous support over a longer time, learning from pilot operations, and scaling up successful projects. The World Bank's rural development strategy, *Reaching the Rural Poor*, has identified several major areas for scaling up. They cover the main factors involved in improving productivity: access to land and water, technology, and finance. Other donors have similar and complementary objectives, summarized here.

(box continued next page)

(box continued)

- **Identifying innovative investments:** A number of new and exciting
  approaches are being piloted for the development and dissemination of
  science and technology, risk management, payment for environmental
  services, and agribusiness development. Many are described throughout this report.

Despite the clear links between agricultural growth and poverty reduction, international and national support for agricultural development
declined steadily from about 1980 to 2000. Only recently has it showed
signs of recovering. Official development assistance (ODA) for agriculture provided by the Organisation for Economic Co-operation and Development (OECD) countries and unilateral agencies fell from US$9.4 billion
in 1980 to US$3.5 billion in 2000. Development assistance declined in rel-
ative terms as well, from 18 percent of total assistance by OECD countries
in 1980 to 7 percent in 2002.[1] Similarly, World Bank funding for agriculture (unadjusted for inflation) fell from about US$2.5 billion per year in
the early 1990s to less than US$1.0 billion in 2001, before recovering to
US$1.5 billion in 2004.

Even more disturbingly than the decrease in international support,
most developing countries have reduced their share of spending on agriculture. In a sample of 43 developing countries, the share of agriculture in
total government spending declined from 12 percent in 1980 to 9 percent
in 1998. This decline was justified in countries experiencing rapid economic growth and strong structural transformation of agriculture, but
elsewhere it is especially worrisome. It is a particular concern in Sub-
Saharan Africa, where agriculture must serve as the main engine of
growth, but where the share of the public budget allocated to agriculture
dropped from 6.5 percent in 1980 to 4.1 percent in 2000 (Fan and Rao
2003).

There are some signs that a turning point may have been reached at
last. Recent increases in ODA for agriculture, particularly from the World
Bank, Canada, and the United States, are encouraging, and interest in
supporting agricultural development appears to be growing again at the
national level. African governments have made a strong commitment to
double the level of public funding for agricultural development within 10
years, from about US$2.3 billion per year at present to US$4.5 billion per
year in 2013. The myriad forces that influence allocations of development

resources make it difficult to identify the precise reasons for agriculture's sudden resurgence in the development agenda, although several factors appear to be at work:

- greater awareness that agricultural growth can contribute significantly to reducing poverty and malnutrition and sustaining the environment;
- increasing national and local commitment to the policies and investments that are implemented; and
- a wider array and more flexible range of financial instruments and development tools that have become available to support agriculture.

If the past is any guide, however, it will be challenging to maintain the momentum in increasing support to agriculture. The sheer complexity of agricultural development, especially the lack of obvious and standard approaches for investing in agriculture, has often led to rather fickle support from international and national policy makers. Given that agriculture is integral to achieving many of the targets of the MDGs, what can be done to ensure that agriculture remains prominent in the development agenda in the coming years? This chapter looks at ways of improving the quality of investments in agriculture, refining the process through which resources are allocated to agriculture, enhancing and expanding the impact of agricultural investments, and identifying new areas of investment that are consistent with the new realities of agriculture in developing countries.

Improving Investments in Agriculture

Four interlocking actions will largely define the rate, volume, and quality of investments in agricultural development. They are (1) improving agricultural stakeholders' participation in the policy dialogue, (2) tailoring proposed investments to prevailing funding instruments, (3) enhancing the impact of agricultural investments, and (4) identifying innovative investments. These actions are detailed below.

Improving Agricultural Stakeholders' Participation in the Policy Dialogue

Over the past decade, the process for allocating development funds has changed markedly. Especially with respect to low-income countries, donor agencies have gradually (although not yet completely) adopted a process in which broad-based consultation and policy dialogue are the basis for deciding how to allocate resources. Poverty Reduction Strategy Papers

(PRSPs), the major policy and priority-setting documents in low-income countries, are prepared on the basis of just such broad-based consultations.

Although consultative decision making is a great improvement on the previous purely donor-driven process, it makes setting priorities more dependent on the political economy within countries, in which agricultural stakeholders are notoriously underrepresented. A survey covering the PRSP process in 32 countries shows that agricultural stakeholders are often well represented in the preparatory phases when issues are diagnosed and studied, but their involvement in actually setting priorities is much weaker. For this reason, a critical first step in getting agriculture back on national investment agendas is to strengthen national stakeholders' participation in decision-making processes for agriculture. Four key steps must be taken to ensure that stakeholders are adequately prepared and well represented at the appropriate time:

- *Strengthening ministries of agriculture:* Capacity building in agricultural ministries is critical. The staff in ministries of agriculture is often biased toward technical skills and generally ineffective in interacting with economists, social scientists, and technical specialists from other sectors. Their capacity to interact must be strengthened if they are to represent agriculture effectively in the political economy surrounding decisions on priorities for policy and investment. Moreover, agricultural issues now involve multiple ministries, from environment to trade and health, and a major challenge in developing and implementing a strategy is to ensure support across these ministries as well as the support of their counterpart departments in donor and development banks.
- *Supporting agricultural producer and processor organizations:* Professional organizations can be powerful pressure groups in setting the policy agenda, as seen throughout the developed world. In the policy dialogue with the government, these groups can be a strong force for ensuring that agricultural policies benefit the poor (as long as they focus on improving efficiency and opening markets rather than on protectionism, which has often been the case). Support for professional agricultural organizations is growing throughout the development community; for example, it is the mainstay of French and Danish ODA. The World Bank has incorporated producer organizations in about half of its agricultural investment operations, but it has involved them less in sector strategy development or as agents of change in the policy arena. A significant challenge and opportunity for the international community, particularly for international financial institutions, is to find new ways to help farmers and small-scale processors represent their interests in policy discussions.

- *Supporting the preparation of national agricultural strategies to develop a common vision and consistent purpose across the sector and among major stakeholders:* A document defining the main policies, institutions, and investments; their priority and sequencing; and arrangements for implementation and monitoring can be a rallying point for agriculture at the national level. It also serves to focus and coordinate donor and government activities for the greatest impact, as in Tanzania (chapter 1, box 1.2).

- *Informing policy makers with appropriate analytical material and exposing them to alternative policy options:* Good analytical work can lead to more and better treatment of agricultural issues in the policy debate, which in turn can result in more and better investments. Analytical work can include specific studies to determine key constraints on policy and investment at the macroeconomic or sector level—for example, economic sector work—as well as workshops on policy issues, study tours, or other means of gathering and assessing information. Less formal approaches, especially when based on mutual respect between policy analyst and policy maker, have proven very effective in influencing policy agendas. Another type of analytical study is the public expenditure review, which assesses the efficiency and equity of public investments by governments and external agencies. An expenditure review can be a powerful tool to identify gaps, inefficiencies, and imbalances in public expenditure. Despite the importance of these analyses in providing the basis for sound policy and investment decisions, funding for such work is limited. Policy groups in ministries of agriculture generally are weak and underfunded. Local economic research institutes and universities, although gaining in significance, still lack the skills for comprehensive work. Funding for economic sector work by international finance institutions and bilateral agencies, such as the World Bank, has picked up slightly after declining to less than 1 percent of annual investments, but it remains inadequate to support sustained, high-quality lending.

Tailoring Investments to Prevailing Funding Instruments

The typical investment project of the 1980s and 1990s, with detailed descriptions of inputs and expected outputs, has been succeeded by a variety of funding arrangements, varying from the classical investment projects to budgetary support and sectorwide support programs. Cofinancing between different sources of funding has become increasingly important. The principal attributes of the various funding instruments, their negative and positive features for agricultural development, and the main entry points are detailed in annex 2.

Different funding instruments are required (and used) as a particular innovation moves from the experimental stage to piloting, introducing and disseminating good practices, scaling up, and on to widespread adoption. For example:

- To pilot innovative concepts and ideas, learning and innovation loans (LILs) and adjustable program loans (APLs) are the most suitable instruments.
- To disseminate a good practice to a larger area, sector investment loans (SILs), eventually integrated in a sectorwide approach (SWAp) are the most suitable vehicles.
- To sustain national- or regional-level practices, which do not require earmarked funding, or to support changes in institutions and policies, programmatic lending instruments, such as programmatic sector adjustment loans (PSALs) and poverty reduction support credits (PRSCs) are the main instruments.[2] They provide direct budgetary support for implementing an agreed-upon program with targets that are consistent with Poverty Reduction Strategies or Country Assistance Strategies. They provide short-term (one-year) guaranteed funding, without targeting or earmarking specific investments. The broad nature of programmatic lending means that decisions on allocating resources by sector are quite dependent on the political economy of a country. If they are widely endorsed by stakeholders, these instruments can be quite successful, as shown in box 6.1.

Currently investments in the agricultural sector are financed mostly through the more conventional sector investment instrument. Over the fiscal period 2001/03, 75 percent of World Bank agricultural lending consisted of well-conscribed investment lending, with only a slight increase in programmatic lending in fiscal 2004.

Although the integration of agricultural investments into programmatic lending is often discussed, two basic concerns remain. The first concern is the short-term nature of the support. In principle, subsequent programmatic loans are expected to focus on the same area(s), so programmatic lending could cover some longer-term investments, such as infrastructure, institutional development, and capacity building. Despite several positive cases in which programmatic lending has consistently supported particular sectors (including the agricultural sector, as in Albania, Tanzania, and Uganda), it is more common for subsequent loans to focus on different sectors or on different concerns within a sector. When continuity is lacking, programmatic lending will be suitable

---

**Box 6.1 Bulgaria: Broad-Based Adjustment Lending
to Improve Policies for Agriculture**

The World Bank funded two agricultural programmatic sector adjustment
loans (PSALs) in Bulgaria to make agriculture more efficient and generate
rural employment by developing an active land market, privatizing the
grain marketing agency and processing firms, limiting the operations of
State Grain Reserves, privatizing irrigation systems by decentralizing
management and maintenance to water user associations (WUAs),
improving agricultural financing, liberalizing trade, and improving market regulations.

The full support of the elected government and the World Bank's will-
ingness to make adjustments in response to the government's perceived
risks were both important to success. Timely, high-quality sector work
involved stakeholders and built consensus to support difficult reforms,
and appropriately timed support (including disengagement in periods
when the policy environment was poor) helped to increase the credibility
and overall effectiveness of the lending program. Several challenges
remain, however, including revitalizing the privatized agro-enterprises
and WUAs, stimulating land markets and rural finance, and improving
export quality.

Source: World Bank 2004b.

---

only for meeting short-term needs, such as support for policy changes.
In any case, for a development program to be successful and comprehensive, programmatic lending has to be combined with investment
lending.

The second concern with using programmatic lending for agricultural
investments is the disparity between recommendations in the diagnostic
phase and the priority themes covered in the PRSCs. A recent survey
found that two-thirds of PRSC actions did not have an adequate founda-
tion in the PRSP diagnostic discussion (box 6.2).

Just as the financial instruments for international investments have
changed, so has the focus of those investments. The last decade has seen
a much greater emphasis on investments in public goods such as science
and technology, information management and dissemination, the development of regulatory systems, and environmental protection. In agriculture, these areas have relatively low—although continuing—funding
requirements. Even in a "hardware" sector, such as infrastructure for
agriculture (irrigation, rural roads), the emphasis has changed from making new investments to supporting operation and maintenance. New

---

Box 6.2 It (Sometimes) Pays to Participate: Representation in the PRSP Process Can Lead to Increased Support

In **Kenya**, the Pastoral Forum (the national association of nomadic live-stock keepers), participating in a group focusing on themes of interest to pastoralists, has been active in formulating the interim and final Poverty Reduction Strategy Papers (PRSPs). The need for investments to benefit the poor in arid and semi-arid pastoral areas was articulated clearly in the interim PRSP and translated into support for the second phase of the World Bank–funded Arid Land Natural Resource Management project. Investments in larger roads and infrastructure not covered under the credit were also identified and prioritized.

In **Mozambique,** a rural strategy was developed through consultation with prospective beneficiaries in seminars and national and local meet-ings. The consultation took advantage of a participatory network that had already been developed under the multidonor–funded Agricultural Investment Program (PROAGRI) project. PROAGRI also organized the-matic consultations involving discussions on priorities for the cashew, cot-ton, and sugar sectors. Improved pest control, production, multiplication and distribution of improved seed for these crops, as well as improved extension services to disseminate technology and information, all figured prominently in the PRSP. The share of the state budget allocated to agri-culture increased by about 60 percent, and the number of field demonstra-tions increased by 10 percent.

In **Vietnam,** exemplary rural participation in the poverty assessment did not immediately translate into additional investment. A poverty task force (initially set up to facilitate government-donor-NGO collaboration on poverty issues) became the main mechanism for coordinating partici-patory poverty assessments and community consultations. Remote rural communities and other poor, disadvantaged communities were repre-sented in the consultations, which helped develop detailed policy propos-als and influenced a policy shift in favor of poor, disadvantaged groups, including the rural poor. The resulting PRSP reflects a greater emphasis on land issues; the delivery of rural health, education, and agricultural sup-port services; and the diversification of production. Of the first two Poverty Reduction Support Credits (PRSCs) that followed, however, the first paid only limited attention to agricultural support services, and the second paid none whatsoever. Similarly, productivity inputs (i.e., technol-ogy, seed, and fertilizer), which received priority in the PRSP, were not covered in subsequent PRSCs.

A recent study of **32 countries** in which agriculture was covered ade-quately in PRSPs has identified a significant disparity between the depth and quality of the poverty diagnosis in the PRSP and the extent to which these issues have translated into priority investments. Among the 12 countries that had follow-up PRSCs, 72 (38 percent) of 189 rural priority

---

(box continued)
activities included in PRSP action matrices were taken up in the
approved or planned PRSCs. An additional 117 (62 percent) were not
included. Even when all funding vehicles (government and international)
are included, 32 percent of the priority activities are not supported by
investments.

Additional work is clearly needed to determine why analytical work
and stakeholder intervention succeed or fail to improve the quality and
volume of lending. Is the analytical work done well and at the right time?
Is the quality of stakeholders' involvement good? Perhaps even more
importantly, is the resulting information disseminated through the most
appropriate channels at the most appropriate time? The political economy
surrounding decisions on priorities for policy and investment is also likely
to play a very important role in ministries of finance in the developing
world, international finance institutions, and donor agencies. Unfamiliar-
ity with the agricultural sector, as well as personal likes and dislikes, can
also strongly influence support for the sector.

Source: World Bank internal documents.

---

investments with these public good characteristics therefore must be
identified (see below).

Enhancing the Impact of Agricultural Investments

Agricultural projects generally have higher costs of preparation and
supervision, and slower disbursement, than investments in other sectors.
In the World Bank, agricultural investment projects cost about 30 percent
more per dollar invested than projects in other sectors. Agricultural
investment projects are also criticized for being "enclave operations"; in
other words, they produce good results in a discrete area with a limited
number of beneficiaries, but they cannot be replicated on a large
(national) scale and so cannot make a real impact on the livelihoods of
millions of rural poor. These characteristics discourage donors from consistently promoting investments in agriculture. Moreover, projects in agriculture have generally been viewed as performing below the level of
those in other sectors, although more recently performance has improved
and is now similar to that of other sectors.

To get agriculture back on the development agenda, it is essential to increase
the poverty reduction impact (i.e., the number of poor reached and poverty alle-
viation effect) per unit of investment. Four approaches can help to achieve
that goal: reducing project preparation costs, using umbrella project

designs, scaling up good practice, and maintaining and improving the quality of the investments.

Reducing project preparation costs: The current operational framework offers relatively few opportunities for cutting preparation costs. The most important opportunity is to ensure that successful projects are scaled up.

One reason that is often cited for the higher preparation costs of agricultural investments is the higher number of environmental and social safeguards that are required. This issue can be addressed by moving the safeguard assessment up from the project to the national level, and by relying more on national capabilities to reduce costs.

There is no escaping the fact that agricultural development is complex and multisectoral, with multiple support and entry points that target a highly varied and widely dispersed population of beneficiaries. For this reason, projects must be developed and implemented through a process (usually involving lengthy, resource-demanding consultations) that is likely to vary for each project, rather than through a straightforward series of steps that can be applied uniformly to each project. Cutting back on the process would cause the quality of agricultural operations to fall to the level of the 1980s.

Using umbrella project designs: Under an umbrella project, a general framework defines the criteria for eligibility for support to a specific country, and so reduces the costs of processing subsequent investments. Examples include the AIDS programs in Africa and the Caribbean, disaster management in the Caribbean, and the African Agricultural Productivity Program (AAPP) for Africa (box 6.3). Although the key requirement for an umbrella design, that is, universal application of a concept, might be difficult to fulfill in the complex environment of agricultural development, some activities, such as agricultural research and land registration, might meet these conditions.

Scaling up good practice: Another way to increase efficiency is to increase the number of beneficiaries by scaling up from "enclave" projects to broad-based agricultural development investments, thus decreasing the unit cost per beneficiary reached. *Reaching the Rural Poor* has identified several areas for scaling up. Summarized in table 6.1, these areas cover the main factors involved in improving productivity: access to land and water, technology, and finance. Other donors have similar objectives and also focus on empowerment, water, and partnerships with the private sector (annex 1). Although regions clearly differ in their resource endowments and priorities, these productivity-enhancing factors have broad applicability and are already a major tool for getting agriculture back on the development agenda.

While scaling up good practice is the primary tool for increasing impact and reducing costs, the danger inherent in promoting an intervention pre-

---

Box 6.3 AAPP: Adapting Donor Procedures to Get African Agriculture Research Moving Again

The African Agricultural Productivity Program (AAPP) seeks to support African agriculture through investments that improve the effectiveness and efficiency of agricultural technology generation, dissemination, and adoption. AAPP would provide resources for research at the subnational, national, regional, and international levels. To foster innovation, it would promote pluralistic, demand-driven agricultural research systems. AAPP is strongly supported by the New Partnership for Africa's Development (NEPAD). To cut preparation costs and time, it has been proposed that a common structure and monitoring and evaluation criteria (for both the country-specific and the regional components) should be developed. The subsequent country-specific operations would be developed within this framework. Such an approach would enhance links between projects and countries, as well as the cost-benefit ratio of project preparation and supervision.

Source: World Bank internal documents.

---

maturely on a wide scale, without evaluating its long-term social and physical sustainability, is very real. The danger of pursuing a one-size-fits-all approach is also considerable, leading to oversimplified and thus poorly adapted and unsustainable investments. Experience with the unsustainable Training and Visit Extension system in Sub-Saharan Africa and South Asia, and with the Integrated Rural Development model worldwide, should be instructive for the future.

Maintaining and improving the quality of the investments: In recent decades, the quality of externally funded agricultural operations has improved significantly, as shown by evaluations of completed projects by DFID, IFAD, and the World Bank. The key lessons from these evaluations can be summarized as follows:

- Projects give the best results when they have a simple and flexible design, simple and measurable development objectives, and a strong commitment from borrowers.
- Institutional development and the sustainability of projects remain weak and must be improved.
- The effectiveness of investments in reducing poverty must be improved. More attention must be given to undertaking comprehensive poverty assessments and to designing projects based on wide consultation to ensure that the poor truly benefit.

Table 6.1 Important Agricultural Productivity Investment Areas for Scaling Up

Area	Investment item	Key enabling requirements	Successful examples of scaled up activities	Preferred Instruments
Land administration; policy and markets	Land administration and reform	Appropriate legal framework	East European and Central Asia region, Brazil, Mexico	SIL followed by PSAL and PRSC to maintain systems
Sustainable natural resource management (NRM) for agriculture	NRM activities in watersheds, wetlands	Community organization and decentralization	Indonesia, Turkey, India, Brazil, Tunisia, Morocco	SIL with a community-driven development (CDD) approach
Irrigation and drainage	Water user association; organization and maintenance systems	Clearly defined water rights	Central Asia, India, Pakistan	SIL with a CDD approach
Science and technology	Competitive research grants	Strong multi-institutional framework for R&D, strong links with CGIAR research centers	Colombia, Peru, China	SIL
Extension and information services	Demand-driven extension services	Farmers and commodity organizations	Sub-Saharan Africa, Latin America	SIL, at national level to be integrated in PRSC/PSAL
Rural finance	Low-cost delivery systems for microfinance	Appropriate overall framework of the financial sector	Albania, Latvia, Egypt, Indonesia	PRSC/PSAL to establish framework, followed by SIL

Source: World Bank internal documents

- Simpler but more relevant monitoring and evaluation systems are needed to improve documentation of the effects of agricultural development operations. Monitoring and evaluation systems have been weak because few projects have the resources to conduct adequate baseline surveys, because key monitoring indicators often do not reflect the project's main objectives, and because data collection systems are not sufficiently attuned to the analytical and decision-making capacity of agricultural policy makers. A recent review of World Bank agricultural projects showed that only 41 percent had adequate monitoring and evaluation plans.

A final challenge is to learn more from others in the development community about measures to improve the quality and impact of projects and integrate this knowledge into a wider number of donor-funded operations. The Global Donor Platform for Rural Development, which brings together the major donors in a broad-based global coalition to reduce rural poverty, is an important mechanism for achieving this goal. The Platform focuses on knowledge sharing and learning, on the impact of agriculture on meeting the MDGs, and on joint support for preparing national rural development strategies. As shown in annex 1, the donor community's rural strategies reflect a consensus that agricultural growth is central to reducing poverty. The Platform will be an important instrument for broadening this understanding by sharing knowledge and experiences and raising awareness of the effectiveness of agricultural development.

Identifying Innovative Investments in Agriculture

At the same time that a major effort is being mounted to bring good practice up to national scale, the agricultural development community must develop new investment activities and identify new ways of channeling investment funds for agricultural development.

Investment areas: Table 6.2 summarizes important investment areas for pilot testing, describes some of the conditions for success, and lists successful ventures.

Matching grants and other support: Matching grants have been described in detail in chapter 4. To recapitulate, they are useful for activities with:

- a high potential to reduce poverty, because they focus on specific (marginal) areas or address issues that are particularly relevant to the poor, such as access to land and water, the reduction of risk and vulnerability,

Table 6.2 Important Investment Areas for Pilot Testing

Area	Detailed investment item	Key enabling requirements	Successful pilots
Science and technology	Commercializing research products	Different institutions already operating	Peru, China
	Financing multicountry research systems	Strong regional research networks	Research networks in Africa
	Biotechnology	Skilled staff, careful selection of area (to avoid overlapping with private sector), and adequate biosafety framework	India, Brazil
Extension and information services	Greater use of information and communications technology by farmers, particularly women	Infrastructure	Russia, India
Sustainable natural resource management for agriculture	Paying for environmental services	Commitment of national and global community to pay for global benefits produced by farming	Costa Rica
Agribusiness and market development	Introducing chain management, strengthening food safety institutions	Physical and market potential to produce high-quality, perishable products	China, Balkan countries
Management of agricultural risk, vulnerability, and disasters	Commodity and price risk management	Adequate banking systems	Tanzania, El Salvador (for coffee)
	Crop and livestock risk insurance	Adequate insurance institutions	Morocco, Mongolia

and specific agricultural activities such as small-livestock production and cottage industries;
* sizable ancillary benefits, such as training, technology development, access to information, project preparation, participation in trade fairs, investment in local infrastructure, and collective action for mutual benefit with spillover effects (van der Meer 2004).

Working more closely with private partners: Complementary funding from institutions focused on the public and private sector (e.g., funding from the World Bank and the IFC) would help to harness the synergies between the public and the private sector and increase overall levels of investment. Differences in approval procedures, the time required for approval, and the specific funding instruments involved have made such cooperation difficult. Recently, however, a number of positive examples have emerged, especially for new areas of investment, in which the World Bank elaborated the basic conceptual framework and the IFC provided most of the investments (box 6.4).

Conclusions: Increasing Impact and Getting Agriculture Back on the Development Agenda

International and national public funding for agriculture have begun to recover after a decline lasting slightly more than two decades. This decline occurred even in countries where agriculture could be the major engine of growth. Although prospects for funding look favorable, there is no guarantee that increased support can be maintained over the longer term. In this context of scarce funding, careful attention must be given to enhancing the impact of agricultural investments and the awareness of agriculture's role in reducing poverty and achieving the MDGs.

Decisions on resource allocation are, for the most part, no longer made through a process driven solely by donors and central governments, and they now rely on broad-based consultation and policy dialogue. Even so, the participation of agricultural stakeholders has not necessarily translated into higher priority for agricultural policies and investments. Nor has sound analytical work in the planning phase ensured that corresponding agricultural investments will be made when projects are implemented. Four key steps must be taken to ensure that stakeholders are adequately prepared and well represented at the appropriate time: strengthening capacity in ministries of agriculture and related ministries; supporting producer and processor organizations; supporting the preparation of national agricultural strategies; and informing policy makers.

Box 6.4 IFC–World Bank Cooperation: Innovative Investments Benefit from the Experience of the Public and Private Sector

Close collaboration between the IFC and the World Bank in new and innovative areas, such as weather risk insurance and warehouse receipt financing, provides new channels for public and private institutions to invest jointly in development. Learning from initial work by the International Food Policy Research Institute, which was partially sponsored by the World Bank Group's Development Marketplace program, the World Bank conducted analytical work on the potential for weather risk insurance in Mexico and Morocco. This work was the basis for the IFC's Global Weather Risk Facility, and the Moroccan Weather Risk Management Company has emerged as the first market insurance company to offer weather index insurance on a commercial basis to banks and farmers. In Zambia, the concept of weather-based insurance has been combined with a credit scheme based on warehouse receipts. The IFC and national banks participate, and the World Bank has done the analytical work and is piloting the activities. In all cases, collaboration was based on a clear understanding of the comparative advantages of the IFC and the World Bank, the presence of a strong proponent of this collaboration within the Bank, and varying levels of shared responsibility as the ivestment was developed, as illustrated below.

Schematic Illustration of IFC–World Bank Cooperation Throughout the Project Development Cycle

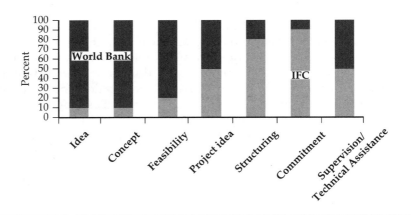

Another means of improving the impact of agricultural investments is to ensure that they are adapted to the much broader set of funding instruments that is now available. A number of new and exciting approaches are being piloted for the development and dissemination of science and technology, risk management, payment for environmental services, and agribusiness. Much can also be achieved by reducing project preparation costs, ensuring that programmatic funding is used to provide continuous support over a longer time, learning from pilot operations, and scaling up successful projects.

Finally, the agricultural sector can command greater attention by clearly communicating the impact of agricultural investments on economic growth and the welfare of the poor. By improving the monitoring and evaluation of agricultural investments, it is possible to understand the magnitude of their impact and to improve future investments. By sharing this information more widely, the development community will increase the likelihood that more and better investments are made in agriculture, that the world comes closer to attaining the MDGs, and that public awareness of agriculture's contributions to achieving the MDGs improves.

Annex 1 Rural Strategies of Other Donor Agencies and Regional Development Banks

Theme	United States Agency for International Development (USAID)	Ministry for Foreign Affairs of Finland (MFAF)	Canadian International Development Agency (CIDA)	Ministry of Foreign Affairs–Norway	U.K. Department for International Development (DFID)	European Union–Directorate General for Development (EU)	Inter-American Development Bank (IADB)	African Development Bank (AfDB)	Asian Development Bank (ADB)
Natural resource management (NRM)	Integrated NRM with focus on water	Water, soil, biological diversity, and agricultural intensification	Shared natural resources and cross-border problems; land degradation	NRM with focus on women, grassroots organizations	Soil and water, degraded land; participatory approach	Equitable access to land	Water and watershed management	Effective innovations and implementation of land tenure	Soil and water degradation; local institutions for watershed management
Knowledge and technology	Training, outreach and adaptive research; support biotechnology	Participatory research; extension and training for poor farmers	Productivity; create and share knowledge; capacity with biotechnology	Strengthening research and education (restrictive position on genetically modified organisms)	Investment in knowledge, technology; extension; indigenous knowledge	Equitable access to productive assets, markets, and services	Diversify public services and increase innovative systems	Innovative extension services and indigenous knowledge	Science and technology; partnership with the private sector
Private sector development	Local and global partnerships for food processing and food safety	Rural livelihoods; capacity in trade negotiations	Develop well-functioning markets; capacity building, networking, and exchange	Promote market development; improve developing countries' market access	Strengthening regulations (improving food safety and quality)	Capacity building for food safety, food standards, and marketing	Risk management, regulation/support for private banking and rural microenterprises	In rural finance, the delivery of inputs/services, storage, processing, and marketing	In service provision, process, marketing, storage, infrastructure, and finance

Investments in infrastructure and social/human development	Support for social equity and human rights; impact of HIV/AIDS on labor supply	Manage international migration, food security	Food security especially in Africa; basic services to land/water; poor people's rights to land/water	Roads, water supply, equitable access to land, resources, managing poor's vulnerability/risk, impact of HIV/AIDS	Health/nutrition education; population, water, and sanitation; manage risks; safety nets; equity in infrastructure	Develop human resources, rural infrastructure, land markets, and land tenure	Focus on road networks and water (drinking water and irrigation)	Focus on water delivery and transport
Community development and empowerment	Empower poor and women	Empower local communities, women	Focus on community approaches to natural resource management	Participatory approach; capacity building and sustainability of local organizations	Address the social and political exclusion of the rural poor	Focus on marginal areas	Build capacity for decentralized units and empower communities	Local institutions for watershed management and NRM
Broad-based rural growth and national ownership	Support of national ownership; enable political and economic operating environment		Coordinate policy areas at the national and international level	Improve rural livelihoods through broad-based development support	Promote broad-based rural economic growth; perform supporting stand-alone projects	Consolidate economic reform for poverty reduction within stable macroeconomic framework		

Sources: ADB 2002; AfDB 2002; CIDA 2003; DFID 2003; EU-DG Development 2000; IADB 2000; MFAF 2004; and USAID 2004.

Annex 2 Key Characteristics of the Main Financial Development Instruments

Programmatic lending: Support for a defined medium-term program, with a phased series of loans or credits, based on completed policy/structural reforms funding balance of payments support with a negative list

Funding instrument	Key characteristics	Positive attributes for agricultural investments	Negative attributes for agricultural investments	Action and entry points
Poverty Reduction Support Credit (PRSC)	Multidonor program to support the country's poverty reduction program. In the World Bank, subject to "soft" loans (IDA) only. Emphasis on support for social sector and on fiduciary institutions (e.g., accountability, decentralization). Fast disbursing, not earmarked, limited due-diligence requirements (safeguards, audits, procurement).	The poverty focus of PRSCs would lead to a strong rural focus, as poverty is most prevalent in rural areas. PRSC programmatic funding should make it particularly suitable for support to already mainstreamed activities.	PRSCs are predominantly providing budgetary support for the social sectors. Although in principle intended to provide medium-term, sustained funding support to one sector, they often are used to cover short-term, recurrent costs, which makes them less suitable for long-term agricultural investments, such as infrastructure and capacity building.	• Well-timed preparation of analytical work, to ensure convincing case for policy-supported programmatic lending. • Better integration of the representatives of agricultural sector (public and private sector, civil society) in priority setting and the PRSP process. • A clear action plan that identifies funding areas suitable for PRSC funding. • A strategy for involving agricultural staff in designing the operation.
Programmatic Sector Adjustment Loan or Credit (PSAL/C)	Similar to PRSC, but not linked to PRSP or IDA funding.	Has a pronounced poverty focus like the PRSC, but less likely to be very relevant to the agricultural sector.	Same as above.	Same as above.

168

Adjustable Program Loans (or Credits) (APLs)	Longer-term, phased investment plan, mostly sector based, with long-term objective imbedded in country strategy, and specific short-term goals, which serve as triggers for passing to subsequent phases.	Longer-term nature meets agricultural sector requirements.	Long-term commitment leaves limited room for flexibility. Short-term goals (triggers) are often too ambitious, and cause premature closure, thus defeating the long-term potential value of these funds.	Good analytical work and in-depth dialogue with government to ensure clear understanding and articulation of long-term goals.
Agricultural Investment Loans or Credits (SILs)	Traditional investment vehicle with clearly defined goals and procedures.	Specific investment targeting ensures high-quality preparation and supervision.	Discrete "enclave" type projects often lack local ownership and show poor sustainability. Links with other sectors are weak.	In country dialogue, stress the need for complementarity between SILs and other (programmatic) instruments.
Technical Assistance Loans (TALs)	Mainly advisory services and studies, often accompanying programmatic loans/credits.	With limited capacity in agricultural policy formulation/institutional reform in ministries of agriculture and in	Increased emphasis by clients and the Bank on "results on the ground" and reluctance to borrow funds	As with SILs, stress complementarity with programmatic lending.

(*Annex continued*)

Annex 2 Key Characteristics of the Main Financial Development Instruments (Continued)

Investment lending: Support for specific investments, usually confined to an area or (sub) sector, to be implemented over a clearly defined (5–10 year) period, with expected outputs to be achieved at project completion

Funding instrument	Key characteristics	Positive attributes for agricultural investments	Negative attributes for agricultural investments	Action and entry points
		farmer organizations, this instrument is suited to support programmatic lending.	for technical assistance or studies.	
Learning and Innovation Loans or Credits (LILs)	Shorter and faster approval procedures, restricted funding levels for innovative approaches to agricultural development.	This instrument is ideally suited for small pilot operations in new areas of involvement, such as higher-value crops and environmental services.	Formally faster, with less control from the World Bank, but transactions costs as share of investment still very high.	Develop more thinking on innovative techniques and nurture them; involve the pressure of civil society.

Source: Authors.

Endnotes

Chapter 1

1. In this report, *agriculture* or *the agricultural sector* is defined to include crops, livestock, and aquaculture within a broad commodity chain from production to consumption. *Agriculture* also includes the main natural resources (soil and water) on which agriculture is based and also the social capital and human resources linked to the sector (particularly women's essential role in agriculture).

2. For an extended discussion of these links, see World Bank (2005b).

3. The Nigerian Roots and Tubers Research Institute, in collaboration with the International Institute of Tropical Agriculture (IITA), a member of the Consultative Group on International Agricultural Research (CGIAR).

4. This indicator captures whether children are consuming enough food of sufficient nutritional quality, and it also reflects access to health care, clean water, good sanitation, and other factors that influence good nutritional outcomes for children.

5. The remaining fifth are urban poor; see the Millennium Project Hunger Task Force (2004).

6. See also FAO's Anti-Hunger Programme (2003a) (ftp://ftp.fao.org/unfao/bodies/cfs/cfs29/Y8752e.pdf).

7. This is the baseline scenario used in IFPRI's IMPACT model. In this scenario, slow progress in policy reforms results in slow growth. Projections were estimated based on historical experience with declining rates of public investment in agricultural research and rural infrastructure, and they explicitly accounted for the slowdown in yield growth that has occurred. The methodology used to develop the model relied on ex-post and ex-ante studies of priority setting in agricultural research, studies of growth in agricultural productivity, analysis of the role of industrialization on growth, and "expert opinion" to generate the projected time path of yield growth. Yield growth projections also account for expected effects of environmental degradation on yields. See Rosegrant et al. (2001) for details.

8. For a comprehensive outline of the various targets and indicators associated with each of the eight MDGs, see the MDG website, "Tracking Progress," http://www.undp.org/mdg/trackingprogress.html.

Chapter 2

1. Of the 305 disputes brought to the WTO between 1995 and 2002, countries with per capita incomes under US$800 brought only 18 complaints. The recent

successful challenge of U.S. cotton subsidies by Brazil, Benin, and Chad report-edly cost Brazil US$1 million.

2. *Civil society* refers to organizations that operate to enable citizens to coordi-nate their efforts but are neither part of the state nor part of the market. They include formal and informal associations such as NGOs, trade unions, self-help groups, and producer organizations.

3. One caution may be in order. Some larger (often international) NGOs, having lost the flexibility and grassroots presence that were their hallmarks, may present challenges (and lead to failures) similar to those commonly seen in other large organizations.

Chapter 3

1. *Institutions* are defined as rules and norms that help transmit information, enforce property rights and contracts, coordinate private activities, and promote collective action that reduces transaction costs.

2. The principle of equivalence in food safety is based on the recognition that the same level of food safety can be achieved by applying alternative hazard con-trol measures. Equivalence becomes a useful tool for regulators to ensure the health and safety of consumers without unnecessarily hindering innovation in the food industry.

3. The Harvest Plus program to improve the nutritional content of cereals receives private sector funding (amounting to US$25 million for four years beginning in 2004).

4. To the extent that the rural landless rely for employment on commercial food crop production, raising food prices may benefit them through increased demand for labor. The net effect of increased food prices and employment is not obvious.

5. See details in World Bank (2004c).

6. See examples in Narayanan and Gulati (2002); Rondot, Biénabe, and Collion (2004).

Chapter 4

1. Detailed investment notes can be found in World Bank (2004b).

2. *Social capital* relates largely to empowerment (as described in chapters 2 and 3) and encompasses relationships and social networks, trust, good will, loyalty, a sense of belonging, understanding, inclusion, engagement, and the structure of the rela-tions between and among individuals and groups.

3. Fortunately, newer and more efficient technologies, such as satellite imaging and geographic information systems, can provide reliable data on changes in the landscape and in land use. With these data, it is easier to determine which partic-ular changes in resource inventory and quality will promote sound management.

Chapter 5

1. Agricultural production contexts are also distinguished by governance, which is incontestably important but not included in the discussion here.

2. Naturally there is considerable variation within each of these systems, and the approaches recommended in this chapter must be adapted to the specific conditions of individual systems.

3. This classification does not fit agricultural systems in the countries covered by the Europe and Central Asia (ECA) region of the World Bank. Systems in ECA tend to have reasonable production potential, reasonable infrastructure, and good access to markets. Because these countries are further along in the transformation process, agriculture is becoming or has become a relatively small part of the national economy. The major challenges to agriculture in the ECA region are intensification, the consolidation of the farms created through collectivization, the development of market structures, and the promotion of nonfarm economic activities in rural areas.

4. Irrigated high-potential areas are defined here as possessing favorable natural and physical resources, reasonably good infrastructure and market linkages, and a proportion of irrigated land to cultivated land that exceeds 33 percent. A rule of thumb in much of Asia is that the addition of irrigation to previously rainfed areas at least doubles yield, so farms that irrigate at least one-third of their area actually rely on irrigation for at least half of their production.

5. Both off-farm employment and exit can be encouraged through better education, better functioning labor markets (both urban and rural), and improved transportation systems.

6. This section draws heavily on Kelley and Byerlee (2003).

Chapter 6

1. Data represent a three-year average. They include only that assistance that falls under the OECD's classification of ODA.

2. Others, such as structural adjustment loans, rehabilitation loans, and debt reduction loans, are not covered in this chapter.

References

ADB (Asian Development Bank). 2002. "Strategic Framework for ADB Assistance to Agriculture and Rural Development." Paper presented at the Consultation Workshop on the Strategic Framework for ADB Assistance to Agriculture and Rural Development. Available at www.adb.org.

AfDB (African Development Bank). *African Development Report 2002: Rural Development for Poverty Reduction in Africa.* Oxford: Oxford University Press.

Afolami, C., and A. Falusi. 1999. "Effect of Technology Change and Commercialization on Income Equity in Nigeria: The Case of Improved Cassava." Paper presented at International Workshop on Assessing the Impact of Agricultural Research on Poverty Alleviation, San Jose, Cost Rica, September 14–16.

Ali, M., and D. Byerlee. 2002. "Productivity Growth and Resource Degradation in Pakistan's Punjab: A Decomposition Analysis." *Economic Development and Cultural Change* 50(4): 839–63.

Alston, J. M., C. Chan-Kang, M. C. Marra, P. G. Pardey, and T. J. Wyatt. 2000. *A Meta-Analysis of Rates of Return to Agricultural R&D: Ex Pede Herculem?* Research Report 113. Washington, DC: International Food Policy Research Institute.

Anderson, J., and G. Feder. 2004. "Agricultural Extension: Good Intentions and Hard Realities." *The World Bank Research Observer* 19 (1): 41–60.

Ashby, J., A. Braun, T. Garcia, M. Guerrero, L. Hernandez, C. Quiros, and J. Roa. 2001. *Investing in Farmers as Researchers: Experience with Local Agricultural Research Committees in Latin America.* Cali, Colombia: International Center for Tropical Agriculture (CIAT).

Baffes, J., and H. de Gorter. 2005. "Experience with Decoupling Agricultural Support." In M. A. Aksoy and J. C. Beghin, *Global Agricultural Trade and Developing Countries*, ed. M. A. Aksoy and J. C. Beghin, 75–90. Washington, DC: World Bank.

Bauer, C. 2004. *Siren Song: Chilean Water Laws as a Model for International Reform.* Washington, DC: Resources for the Future.

Berdegue, J., and G. Escobar. 2001. "Agricultural Knowledge and Information Systems and Poverty Reduction." AKIS/ART Discussion Paper. World Bank, Rural Development Department, Washington, DC.

Blackden, M., and C. Banu. 1999. *Gender, Growth, and Poverty Reduction, Special Program of Assistance for Africa, 1998 Status Report on Poverty in Sub-Saharan Africa.* World Bank Technical Paper No. 428. World Bank, Washington, DC.

Boselie, B., S. Henson, and D. Weatherspoon. 2003. "Supermarket Procurement Practices in Developing Countries: Redefining the Roles of the Public and Private Sectors." *American Journal of Agricultural Economics,* 85(5): 1155–61.

Brown, L. R., and L. Haddad. 1995. *Time Allocation Patterns and Time Burdens: A Gendered Analysis of Seven Countries.* Washington, DC: International Food Policy Research Institute.

Byerlee, D., and G. Alex. 2002. *Designing Investments in Agricultural Research for Enhanced Poverty Impacts.* Sustainable Agricultural Systems, Knowledge and Information (SASKI) Good Practice Note, World Bank, Washington, DC.

Byerlee, D., and K. Fischer. 2002. "Accessing Modern Science: Policy and Institutional Options for Agricultural Biotechnology in Developing Countries." *World Development* 30 (6): 931–48.

Byerlee, D., and C. Jackson. 2005. *Agriculture, Rural Development and Pro-Poor Growth.* Draft paper, Agriculture and Rural Development Department, World Bank, Washington, DC.

Chadha, G., and A. Gulati. 2002. "Performance of Agro-based Industrial Enterprises in Recent Years: The Indian Case." Paper presented at the "South Asia Initiative Workshop on Agricultural Diversification in South Asia," Bhutan, November 21–23.

CGAP (Consultative Group to Assist the Poorest). 2004. "CGAP Agricultural Microfinance Case Study." Washington, DC: World Bank.

CGIAR (Consultative Group on International Agricultural Research). 2005. "Good News on the CGIAR. A Briefing for the Executive Directors of the World Bank." Prepared for the Committee on Development Effectiveness, 2005. Available at http://www.cgiar.org/.

CIDA (Canadian International Development Agency). 2003. *Promoting Sustainable Rural Development Through Agriculture. Canada Making a Difference in the World.* Available at http://www.rdxxl.org/.

Couture, J. L., and P. Lavigne. 2000. "Institutional Innovations and Irrigation Management in Office du Niger, Mali (1910–1990)." Paper presented at the World Bank Seminar on Institutional Reforms in Irrigation and Drainage, Washington, DC, December 11–12.

Datt, G., and M. Ravallion. 1998. "Farm Productivity and Rural Poverty in India." Food Consumption and Nutrition Division (FCND) Discussion Paper 42, Washington, DC: IFPRI.

de Ferranti, D., G. E. Perry, D. Lederman, A. Valdés, and W. Foster. 2005. *Beyond the City: The Rural Contribution to Development.* Washington, DC: World Bank.

de Gorter, H., and J. Hranaiova. 2004. "Quota Administration Methods: Economics and Effects with Trade Liberalization." In *Agriculture and the WTO: Creating a Trading System for Development*, ed. M. Ingco and D. Nash, 95–118. Washington, DC: World Bank.

de Haan, C., T. S. van Veen, B. Brandenburg, J. Gauthier, F. Le Gall, R. Mearns, and M. Simeon. 2001. *Livestock Development: Implications for Rural Poverty, the Environment, and Global Food Security*. Directions in Development No. 23241, World Bank, Washington, DC.

Delgado, C., M. Rosegrant, H. Steinfeld, S. Ehui, and C. Courbois. 1999. *Livestock to 2020: The Next Food Revolution*. Washington, DC: International Food Policy Research Institute.

DFID (U.K. Department for International Development). 2003. "Agriculture and poverty reduction: unlocking the potential." Available at http://www.rdxxl.org/.

Diao, X., P. Dorosh, and S. Rathman. 2003. "Market Opportunities for African Agriculture: An Examination of Demand Side Constraints on Agricultural Growth." Development Strategy and Governance Division Discussion Paper 1. International Food Policy Research Institute, Washington, DC.

Dixon, J. A., D. P. Gibbon, and A. Gulliver. 2001. *Farming Systems and Poverty: Improving Farmers' Livelihoods in a Changing World*. Rome: Food and Agriculture Organization.

Dolan, C. and J. Humphrey. 2000. *Governance and Trade in Fresh Vegetables: The Impact of UK Supermarkets on the African Horticulture Industry*. University of Sussex, UK: Institute of Developmental Studies.

Dolan, C., and K. Sorby. 2003. "Gender and Employment in High-Value Agriculture Industries." Working Paper 7. World Bank, Agriculture and Rural Development, Washington, DC.

Dorward, A., and J. Kydd. 2002. "The Malawi 2002 Food Crisis: The Rural Development Challenge." Paper presented at a conference to mark the retirement of John McCracken "Malawi after Banda: Perspectives in a Regional African Context," Centre of Commonwealth Studies, September 4–5, University of Stirling.

Dorward, A., J. Kydd, J. Morrison, and I. Urey. 2004. "A Policy Agenda for Pro-Poor Agricultural Growth." *World Development* 32(1): 73–89.

Dugger, C. 2004. "The Food Chain: Survival of the Biggest; Supermarket Giants Crush Central American Farmers." *New York Times*, December 28, 2004.

Eicher, C., 2004. "Rebuilding Africa's Scientific Capacity in Food and Agriculture." Staff Paper 2004-13. Michigan State University, Department of Agricultural Economics, East Lansing, Michigan.

EU-DG Development (European Union—Directorate General for Development). 2000. "Agricultural Sub-Sector Strategy Paper." Available at http://www.rdxxl.org/.

Fan, S., and N. Rao, 2003. "Public Spending in Developing Countries: Trends, Determination, and Impact." Environment, Production and Technology Division Discussion Paper 99. International Food Policy Research Institute, Washington, DC.

Fan, S., P. Hazell, and S. Thorat. 1999. *Linkages between Government Spending, Growth, and Poverty in Rural India.* Research Report No. 110. International Food Policy Research Institute, Washington, DC.

Fan, S., L. Zhang, and X. Zhang. 2002. *Growth, Inequality, and Poverty in Rural China: The Role of Public Investments.* Research Report No. 125. International Food Policy Research Institute, Washington, DC.

FAO (Food and Agriculture Organization). 2003a. *Anti-Hunger Programme.* Report by the Committee on World Food Security. Rome: Food and Agriculture Organization.

_____. 2003b. *World Agriculture: Towards 2015/2030, a Food and Agriculture Organization Perspective.* London, UK: Earthscan Publications, Ltd.

_____. 2004a. *The State of Food and Agriculture—Agricultural Biotechnology: Meeting the Needs of the Poor?* Rome: Food and Agriculture Organization.

_____. 2004b. *The Market for Nontraditional Agricultural Exports.* Rome: Food and Agriculture Organization.

FAOSTAT. 2003. "Food and Agriculture Organization Statistical Databases." Available at http://apps.fao.org/default.htm. (Verified February 24, 2005.)

Feder, G., R. Murgai, and J.B. Quizon. 2004. "Sending Farmers Back to School: The Impact of Farmer Field Schools in Indonesia." *Review of Agricultural Economics* 26(1): 45–62.

Foster, W., and A. Valdés. 2004. *Managing Potential Adverse Impacts of Agricultural Trade Liberalization.* In *Agriculture and the WTO: Creating a Trading System for Development,* ed. Ingco, M., and D. Nash, 193–214. Washington, DC: World Bank.

Fishbein, R. 2001. "Rural Infrastructure in Africa: Policy Directions." Africa Region Working Paper Series Number 18. World Bank, Washington, DC.

Frias, J. 1992. "Evolucion Reciente de la Industria del Agua en Inglaterra, Francia y Chile." SARH, Mexico: McKinsey and Company, Inc.

Gardner, B. 2002. *American Agriculture in the Twentieth Century: How It Flourished and What It Cost.* Cambridge, Massachusetts: Harvard University Press.

Grimble, R., and M. Laidlaw. 2002. *Biological Resource Management: Integrating Biodiversity Concerns in Rural Development Projects and Programs.* Biodiversity Series Paper 85. World Bank, Washington, DC.

Gulliver, A. 2001. *Private Sector-Led Diversification among Indigenous Producers in Guatemala.* In *Global Farming Systems Study: Challenges and*

Priorities to 2030, ed. J. Dixon, A. Gulliver, and D. Gibbon. Washington, DC: World Bank.

Gypmantasiri, P., S. Sriboonchitta, and A. Wiboonpongse. 2001. *Policies for Agricultural Sustainability in Northern Thailand.* London: International Institute for Environment and Development (IIED). Available at http://www.iied.org/sarl/pubs/policieswork.html.

Hagenimana, V., M. Oyunga, J. Low, S. Njoroge, S. Gichuki, and J. Kabira. 1999. *The Effects of Women Farmers' Adoption of Orange-Fleshed Sweet Potatoes: Raising Vitamin A Intake in Kenya.* Research Report Series 3. International Center for Research on Women (ICRW), Washington, DC.

Hazell, P., and C. Ramasamy. 1991. *The Green Revolution Reconsidered: The Impact of High-Yielding Rice Varieties in South India.* Baltimore: The Johns Hopkins University Press.

Hellin, J., and S. Higman. 2002. *Smallholders and Niche Markets: Lessons from the Andes.* Network Paper No. 118. Overseas Development Institute (ODI) Agriculture Research and Extension Network, London, UK.

Henson, S., and W. Mitullah. 2003. "Kenyan Exports of Nile Perch: Impact of Food Safety Standards on an Export-Oriented Supply Chain." Policy Research Working Paper Series No. 3349. World Bank, Washington, DC.

Hess, U. 2003. "Innovative Financial Services for Rural India: Monsoon-Indexed Lending and Insurance for Smallholders." Agriculture and Rural Development Working Paper 9. World Bank, Washington, DC.

Horn, H., and P. Mavroidis. 2003. "Which WTO Provisions Are Invoked by and Against Developing Countries?" Mimeo. Institute for International Economics, Stockholm.

Huang, J., R. Hu, C. Pray, and S. Rozelle. 2002. *Reforming China's Agricultural Research System.* In *Agricultural Research Policy in an Era of Privatization,* ed. D. Byerlee and R. Echeverria, 245–264. Wallingford: CABI Publishing.

Hussain, S., and D. Byerlee. 1995. "Education and Farm Productivity in Post-Green Revolution Agriculture in Asia." In *Agricultural Competitiveness: Market Forces and Policy Choice,* ed. G. H. Peters and D. D. Hedley, 554–69. Aldershot: Dartmouth Publishing Company Limited.

IADB (Inter-American Development Bank). 2000. "Strategy for Agricultural Development in Latin America and the Caribbean." Sustainable Development Department, Washington, DC.

IFAD (International Fund for Agricultural Development). 2004. "Trade and Rural Development. Opportunities and Challenges for the Poor." Discussion Paper. International Fund for Agricultural Development, Rome. Available at http://www.ifad.org/events/gc/27/panel/e.pdf.

IFC (International Finance Corporation). 2004. "IFC Helps Morocco Secure Competitive Private Sector Bids for World's First Public-Private Partnership Irrigation Project." IFC Press Release. Available at http://ifcln001.worldbank.org/.

IFDC (International Fertilizer Development Center). 1994. "Fertilizer Distribution Improvement Project-II." End of Project Report. Ministry of Agriculture, Bangladesh.

_____. 2004. "IFDC Voucher Programs." Draft paper, IFDC, Muscle Shoals, Alabama.

IFPRI (International Food Policy Research Institute). 2002. "Cutting Hunger in Africa Through Smallholder-Led Agricultural Growth." A Technical Paper in Support of USAID's Agricultural Initiative to Cut Hunger in Africa (AICHA). Available at http://www.ifpri.org/themes/ieha/iehatech.pdf. (Verified on February 25, 2005.)

Joffe, S., and S. Jones. 2004. "Stimulating Private Investment and Market Development for Agriculture: New Approaches and Experience." Oxford Policy Management (OPM), Oxford, UK.

Jonakin, J. 1996. "The Impact of Structural Adjustment and Property Rights Conflicts on Nicaraguan Agrarian Reform Beneficiaries." World Development 24 (7):1179–91.

Joshi, P., A. Gulati, P. Birthal, and L. Tewari. 2002. "Agriculture Diversification in South Asia: Patterns, Determinants, and Policy Implications." Markets, Trade and Institutions Division Discussion Paper 57. International Food Policy Research Institute, Washington, DC.

Kelley, T., and D. Byerlee. 2003. "Surviving on the Margin: Agricultural Research and Development Strategies for Poverty Reduction in Marginal Areas." Draft paper Agriculture and Rural Development, World Bank, Washington, DC.

Larson, D., J. Anderson, and P. Varangis. 2004. "Policies on Managing Risk in Agricultural Markets." The World Bank Research Observer 19 (2): 199–230.

López, R. 1996. "Land Titles and Farm Productivity in Honduras." University of Maryland, Department of Agricultural and Resource Economics, College Park, Maryland. Processed.

_____. 2004. "The Structure of Public Expenditure, Agricultural Income and Rural Poverty: The Evidence for Ten Latin American Countries." Research Background Paper prepared for the Tenth Annual World Bank Conference on Rural and National Development in Latin America and the Caribbean, San José, Costa Rica, November 3.

López, R. and G. Anriquez. 2003. "Poverty and Agricultural Growth: Chile in the 1990s." Paper prepared for the Food and Agriculture Organization (FAO) International Conference on the Roles of Agriculture in Developing Countries, Rome, Italy, October 20–22.

Mansuri, G., and V. Rao. 2004. "Community-Based and -Driven Development: A Critical Review." *The World Bank Research Observer* 19 (1): 1–39.

McIntire, J., D. Bourzat, and P. Pingali. 1992. *Crop-Livestock Interaction in Sub-Saharan Africa*. Washington, DC: World Bank.

McKean, M., and E. Ostrom. 1995. "Common Property Regimes in the Forest: Just a Relic from the Past?" *Unasylva*, 46(180): 3–15.

Mellor, J. 2001. "Reducing Poverty, Buffering Economic Shocks—Agriculture and the Non-Tradable Economy." Background Paper prepared for Experts' Meeting, Roles of Agriculture Project, Food and Agricultural Organization (FAO), Rome, March 19–21. Available at www.fao.org/.

MFAF (Ministry for Foreign Affairs of Finland). 2004. "Finland's Rural Development Strategy for International Development." Department for Development Policy. Available at http://global.finland.fi/.

Millennium Project Hunger Task Force (MPHTF). 2004. "Halving Hunger—A Global Programme of Action." Commissioned by the United Nations Development Programme (UNDP).

Minot, N., and M. Ngigi. 2003. "Are Horticultural Exports a Replicable Success Story? Evidence from Kenya and Côte d'Ivoire." Paper presented at the conference organized by Capacity Building International-Germany (InWEnt), the International Food Policy Research Institute (IFPRI), the New Partnership for Africa's Development (NEPAD), and the Technical Centre for Agricultural and Rural Cooperation (CTA) on Successes in African Agriculture. Pretoria, December 1–3.

Munita, J. 1994. "Aumento de Eficiencia en el Uso del Agua por Incorporacion de Nuevas Tecnicas y Arrandmientos Temporales." Universidad de Chile, Santiago.

Narayanan, S., and A. Gulati. 2002. "Globalization and the Smallholders: A Review of Issues, Approaches, and Tentative Conclusions," Markets, Trade and Institutions Division Discussion Paper No. 50. International Food Policy Research Institute (IFPRI), Washington, DC.

OECD (Organisation for Economic Co-operation and Development). 2004. *Agricultural Policies in OECD Countries: Monitoring and Evaluation 2002*. Paris: OECD.

Pardey, P., and N. Beintema. 2001. *Slow Magic: Agricultural R&D a Century after Mendel*. Agricultural Science and Technology Indicators. Washington, DC: International Food Policy Research Institute.

Phillips, D. 2001. *Implementing the Market Approach to Enterprise Support: A Comparative Evaluation of Matching Grant Schemes*. World Bank Policy Research Paper 2589, World Bank, Washington, DC.

Pieri, C., G. Evers, J. Landers, P. O'Connell, and E. Terry. 2002. "No-Till Farming for Sustainable Rural Development." Agriculture and Rural Development Working Paper Series No. 24536. World Bank, Washington, DC.

Pryor, S., and T. Holt. 1999. *Agribusiness as an Engine of Growth in Developing Countries*. Washington, DC: US Agency for International Development (USAID).

Quisumbing, A. 2003. *Household Decisions, Gender, and Development*. Washington, DC: International Food Policy Research Institute/Johns Hopkins University Press.

Raitzer, D. 2003. *Benefit-Cost Meta-Analysis of Investment in the International Agricultural Research Centres of the CGIAR*. Rome: Consultative Group on International Agricultural Research, Science Council.

Ravallion, M., and G. Datt. 1996. "How Important to India's Poor Is the Sectoral Composition of Economic Growth?" *The World Bank Economic Review* 10: 1–26.

Reardon, T., P. Timmer, and J. Berdegue. 2003. "The Rise of Supermarkets in Africa, Asia, and Latin America." *American Journal of Agricultural Economics* 85(5): 1140–6.

Rondot, P., E. Biénabe, and M. H. Collion. 2004. "Rural Economic Organizations and Market Restructuring: What Challenges, What Opportunities for Small Farmers? A Global Issue Paper." Available at http://www.regoverningmarkets.org/.

Rosegrant, M., X. Cai, and S. Cline. 2002. *World Water and Food to 2025: Dealing with Scarcity*. Washington, DC: International Food Policy Research Institute.

Rosegrant, M., M. Paisner, S. Meijer, and J. Witcover. 2001. *Global Food Projections to 2020: Emerging Trends and Alternative Futures*. Washington, DC: International Food Policy Research Institute.

Rosegrant, M., R. Schleyer, and S. Yadav. 1995. "Water Policy for Efficient Agricultural Diversification: Market-Based Approaches." *Food Policy* 20(3): 203–23.

Sadoulet, E., A. de Janvry, and B. Davis. 2001. "Cash Transfer with Income Multiplier: PROCAMPO in Mexico." *World Development* 29(6):1043–56.

Saito, K. 1992. *Raising the Productivity of Women Farmers in Sub-Saharan Africa*. Washington, DC: World Bank, Women in Development Division, Population and Human Resources Department.

Scherr, S., and S. Yadav. 2001. "Land Degradation in the Developing World: Issues and Policy Options for 2020." In *The Unfinished Agenda: Perspectives on Overcoming Hunger, Poverty and Environmental Degradation*, ed. P. Pinstrup-Anderson and R. Pandya-Lorch, 133–138. Washington, DC: International Food Policy Research Institute.

Scoones, I., eds. 1994. *Living with Uncertainty: New Directions in Pastoral Development in Africa*. London: Intermediate Technology Publications.

SIMA (Statistical Information Management & Analysis). World Bank database available at www.worldbank.org/.

Smil, V. 2004. "Food Production and the Environment: Understanding the Challenge, Encountering the Limits, and Reducing the Waste." Paper prepared for the World Bank, Washington, DC, ESSD Week, March 2004, Agriculture and Rural Development sessions.

Spencer, D. 1994. "Infrastructure and Technology Constraints to Agricultural Development in the Humid and Subhumid Tropics of Africa." Environment, Production and Trade Division Discussion Paper No. 3. International Food Policy Research Institute, Washington, DC.

Start, D. 2001. "The Rise and Fall of the Rural Non-Farm Economy: Poverty Impacts and Policy Options." *Development Policy Review* 19(4): 491–505.

Stifel, D., B. Minten, and P. Dorosh. 2003. "Transaction Costs and Agricultural Productivity: Implications of Isolation for Rural Poverty in Madagascar." Markets, Trade and Institutions Division Discussion Paper No. 56. International Food Policy Research Institute, Washington, DC.

Thirtle, C., L. Lin, and J. Piesse. 2003. "The Impact of Research-Led Agricultural Productivity Growth on Poverty Reduction in Africa, Asia, and Latin America." *World Development* 31(12): 1959–75.

Umali, D., L. G. Feder, and C. de Haan. 1994. "Animal Health Services: Finding the Balance between Public and Private Delivery." *World Bank Research Observer* 9(1): 76–9.

UN (United Nations). 2002. *World Population Prospects: The 2002 Revision Population Database.* The United Nations Population Division, New York.

USAID (United States Agency for International Development). 2004. Agricultural Strategy: Linking Producers to Markets. Available at www.usaid.gov/.

USAID (United States Agency for International Development). "Cutting Hunger in Africa through Smallholder-Led Agricultural Growth." Available at www.ifpri.org/.

van der Meer, K. 2002. "Public-Private Cooperation in Agriculture Research: Examples from Netherlands." In *Agricultural Research Policy in an Era of Privatization,* ed. D. Byerlee and R. Echeverria, 123–36. Wallingford: CABI Publishing.

_____. 2004. "Exclusion of Small-Scale Farmers from Coordinated Supply Chains: Market Failure, Policy Failure or Just Economies of Scale." Draft paper. World Bank, Washington, DC.

van der Meer, K., and M. Noordam. 2004. "The Use of Grants in the Market Sector in Rural Development: A Review of World Bank Projects." World Bank, Washington, DC.

Vorley, B. 2001. *The Chains of Agriculture: Sustainability and the Restructuring of Agri-food Markets.* London: International Institute for Environment and Development (IIED).

WEHAB (Water, Energy, Health, Agriculture and Biodiversity) Working Group. 2002. "A Framework for Action on Agriculture." World Summit on Sustainable Development Report. Water, Energy, Health, Agriculture and Biodiversity Working Group, Johannesburg. Processed. August 26–September 2.

World Bank. 2000. *Agriculture in Tanzania Since 1986: Follower or Leader of Growth.* A World Bank Country Study. Washington, DC: World Bank.

————. 2001. *World Development Report 2000/2001: Attacking Poverty.* Washington, DC: World Bank.

————. 2002. *Global Economic Prospects (GEP) and the Developing Countries 2002.* Washington, DC: World Bank.

————. 2003a. *World Development Indicators.* Washington, DC: World Bank.

————. 2003b. *Reaching the Rural Poor: A Renewed Strategy for Rural Development.* Washington, DC: World Bank.

————. 2003c. *The World Bank Group Global Poverty Monitoring.* Washington, DC: World Bank.

————. 2003d. *Global Economic Prospects and the Developing Countries 2003.* Washington, DC: World Bank.

————. 2003e. *Dealing with the Coffee Crisis in Central America: Impacts and Strategies.* Policy Research Working Paper WPS2993. World Bank, Washington, DC.

————. 2003f. *India: Revitalizing Punjab's Agriculture.* New Delhi: World Bank.

————. 2003g. "The CGIAR at 31: An Independent Meta-Evaluation of the Consultative Group on International Agricultural Research," Volume 1. Overview Report. World Bank, Operations Evaluation Department, Washington, DC.

————. 2004a. "Coffee Markets: New Paradigms in Global Supply and Demand." Agriculture and Rural Development Discussion Paper 3. Available at www.worldbank.org/.

————. 2004b. *Agriculture Investment Sourcebook.* Washington, DC: World Bank.

————. 2004c. *Pakistan's Rural Factor Markets: Policy Reforms for Growth and Equity.* Washington, DC: World Bank.

————. 2005a. *Shaping the Future of Water for Agriculture: A Sourcebook for Investment in Agricultural Water Management.* Washington, DC: World Bank.

————. 2005b. *Agriculture and Achieving the Millennium Development Goals.* Washington, DC: World Bank.

————. 2005c. *Food Safety and Agricultural Health Standards: Challenges and Opportunities for Developing Country Exports.* Report No. 31207. World Bank, Washington, DC.

Index

Note: *b* indicates boxes, *t* indicates tables, *f* indicates figures, and *a* indicates annexes.

Eco-Audit

Environmental Benefits Statement

The World Bank is committed to preserving endangered forests and natural resources. We have chosen to print Agricultural Growth for the Poor on 60% post-consumer recycled fiber paper, processed chlorine free. The World Bank has formally agreed to follow the recommended standards for paper usage set by the Green Press Initiative—a nonprofit program supporting publishers in using fiber that is not sourced from endangered forests. For more information, visit www.greenpressinitiative.org.

The printing of these books on recycled paper saved the following:

Trees	Solid Waste	Water	Net Greenhouse Gases	Electricity
10	438	2730	862	1600
	Pounds	Gallons	Pounds	KWH